Elegar
Machine Knits

Elegant MACHINE *Knits*

Valerie Carter

UNWIN
PAPERBACKS

LONDON SYDNEY WELLINGTON

First published in Great Britain by Unwin ® Paperbacks, an
imprint of Unwin Hyman Limited, in 1988.

Unwin Hyman Limited
15–17 Broadwick Street
London W1V 1FP

Allen & Unwin Australia Pty Ltd
8 Napier Street, North Sydney, NSW 2060, Australia

Allen & Unwin New Zealand Pty Ltd with the Port Nicholson Press
60 Cambridge Terrace, Wellington, New Zealand

British Cataloguing in Publication Data

Carter, Valerie
    Elegant machine knits.
    1. Machine knitting-Patterns
    I. Title
    746.43'2041

ISBN 0–04–440249–X

Printed in Portugal by
Printer Portuguesa

Contents

Introduction to machine knitting techniques
Abbreviations

SPRING

Pattern
No

1	Pink Long Sleeve Suit	48
2	Denim Blue Cardigan Suit	50
3	Black-White Fairisle Jacket Suit	54
4	Royal-Blue Rib Dress	57
5	Royal-White Long Line Jacket Suit	59
6	Green-White Batwing Suit	61

SUMMER

7	Turquoise Short Sleeve Suit	63
8	Lemon Short Sleeve Suit	65
9	Mint-Green Summer Dress	68
10	Peach-White Collared Dress	70
11	Blue-White Peplum Cardigan Suit	72
12	Pink Cap Sleeve Top Suit	74

AUTUMN

13	Rust-Brown Fairisle Jacket Suit	76
14	Grey-Heather Buttoned Sweater Suit	80
15	Blue-Heather Cardigan Suit	83
16	Lilac Cowl Neck Suit	85
17	Navy-Blue Zip Jacket Suit	87
18	Grey-Orange Fairisle Sweater Suit	90

WINTER

19	Red Blazer Jacket Suit	93
20	Red-Black Waisted Jacket Suit	96
21	Shades of Blue Woven Jacket Suit	99
22	Shades of Rust Woven Sweater Suit	102
23	Shades of Blue-Claret Woven Mohair Suit	105
24	Shades of Green-Claret Fisherman's Rib Jacket Suit	108

EVENING

25	White Evening Suit	110
26	Black Evening Suit	113
27	Turquoise Motif Top Suit	115
28	Cerise Shift Dress	117
29	White Motif & Bead Suit	119
30	Pink Motif & Bead Suit	123

Postscript	126
List of suppliers	127

Introduction

This book is not intended to teach you to machine knit, there can be no substitute for the instruction book that is supplied with the machine.

It is a book packed full of wearable fashion knitwear that can be worn all the year round and contains a guide to the basic techniques which have been used to knit and finish the patterns.

There are many makes and models of knitting machines on the market and these patterns are suitable for the most popular leading brands of punchcard knitting machines which are available today.

PUNCHCARDS

When knitting a punchcard design from this book, you must make sure that the card is punched so that row one is at the correct starting point for your machine. Row one must be programmed into the machine before the pattern can be knitted.

Some Toyota machines knit the card in reverse so either the yarns need to be changed round or the card punched in reverse.

If the cards are punched out correctly they will work on almost any automatic 24 stitch pattern repeat punchcard knitting machine.

TENSION

These patterns were all knitted on either a 'Jones + Brother', 'Knitmaster' or 'Toyota' punchcard knitting machine. Every machine may vary a little, so all tensions given are only approximate.

Using the correct yarn and tension will not always result in the garment being the correct size, a 4-ply Acrylic in a dark colour will knit up much tighter than a pale colour of the same yarn.

To achieve perfect results it is important to knit a test swatch. The tension dial on the carriage has whole numbers with dots in between the numbers. With some machines it may be necessary to adjust the dial by only one dot, others may vary as much as two or three whole numbers. The only way you can guarantee to achieve the correct tension is to knit a tension swatch, which can be stored for future reference.

KNIT A TEST SWATCH AS FOLLOWS:

If the pattern says MATERIAL: 4-ply
    TENSION: 32 sts × 44 rs = 4ins (10cms)
    T at approx 6

You will need two shades of the 4-ply you are going to knit the garment in. Colour 1, Main Yarn (MY) and colour 2, Waste Yarn (WY).

Cast on more than 70 sts in WY, leaving the 17th stitch each side of centre 0 in Non Working Position (NWP).
* Tension dial (T) at 6.
Knit a few rows in WY.
Change to MY, Knit 44 rs.
Change to WY, Knit 6 rs. *

Repeat from * to * moving the tension dial up or down as required.

Leave the swatch overnight, or for several hours to return to its natural shape. Press the swatch the same way as given in the final making up instructions of the pattern being knitted. Measure the swatch between the ladder created by the missing stitch, to give the number of stitches. It should measure 4ins (10cms). Then measure the distance between the colour changes—that should measure 4ins (10cms) also.

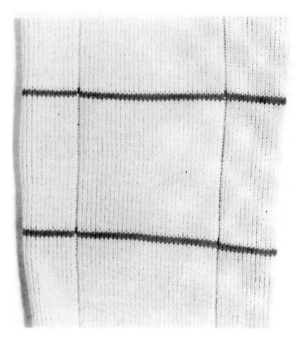

TECHNIQUES

Cast on in Waste Yarn (WY)

This type of cast on is used when hems are being worked or when the ribs or welts are being added later.

WY is yarn that is going to be removed from the main knitting, so it can be different from the yarn used to knit the garment. This is a good way of using up some of those odd yarns, although it is easier to handle if the WY is the same weight as the Main Yarn (MY).

Push forward the required number of needles into Working Position (WP). Thread the carriage with WY. Knit several rows ending with the carriage on the left.

Thread up the nylon cord and knit one row. This separates the waste knitting from the main knitting. (There are several different colours available in nylon ravel cords, so use one of a contrasting colour to make separation easier.)

Change to MY and continue to knit pattern.

WY should not be removed until the garment is finished.

Cast on by hand

This gives a closed edge cast on. It may also be known as 'cast on by hand using the e method'.

Starting with the carriage at the right and with the yarn on the left, bring forward the required number of needles into Holding Position (HP). Secure the yarn with a slip knot around the first needle on the left.

Wind the yarn round each needle in an anticlockwise direction, as if you were making a letter 'e' over each needle. Try not to pull the yarn too tight and to keep the loops even.

When all the needles are wrapped, thread the yarn through the carriage ready to knit. Take up any slack yarn.

With the carriage set to knit back the needles, knit one row. * Push all needles back into HP, knit one row*, repeat from * to * until enough knitting has been produced to enable small claw weights to be hung. Then continue to knit as normal.

When the carriage and yarn are at the left and the pattern says c.on by hand xx number of stitches at the left, unthread the yarn from the carriage, pull the required number of needles into HP and work the c.on in reverse starting at the right and winding the yarn in a clockwise direction, finishing at the left. Re-thread the yarn and work as before.

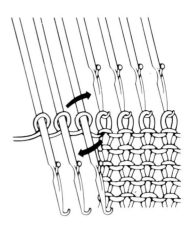

Ribs and Welts

The instructions for the patterns in this book are given for machines with ribbing attachments. For machines without a ribber, the ribs and welts can be worked either in continental rib or by reforming the stitches.

Continental rib

Cast on in WY, 1 x 1, the number of stitches stated in the pattern. Knit a few rows ending with the carriage at the left, knit one row with the nylon cord.

With the MY, and with the tension dial at least three numbers lower than the main tension, work approximately two thirds the number of rows stated in the pattern: i.e. if the pattern says K 30 rows, knit 20 rows for continental rib, knit one row at a large tension—for the folding line—then work the same number of rows at the previous tension.

Turn up hem.

Reformed ribs

Cast on in WY, 1 x 1, the number of stitches stated in the pattern. Leave two needles at the left in WP.

Knit a few rows, ending with the carriage at the left. Knit one row with the nylon cord. Thread the carriage with the MY. With the tension dial at 0, knit four rows.

Insert the transfer tool into the loop of the first row of main knitting, and place it onto the first needle at the left.

Bring forward the empty needles into WP. With the tension dial one tension tighter than the main knitting, knit the required number of rib rows.

Working from the third needle at the left, insert the latch tool/tappet under the first row of the main knitting and reform the stitch with the latch tool.

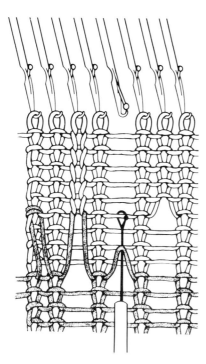

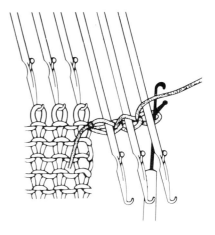

Shaping

When knitting fairisle or stitch patterns, it is not necessary to work fully fashioned shapings. On stocking stitch garments, though, fully fashioned shapings look more professional.

Fully fashioned decrease

This can be worked as many stitches into the work as may be required, but is normally worked two or three needles in.

With a two or three pronged tool, transfer the end stitches onto adjacent needles, leaving the end one empty—push this back to NWP.

Fully fashioned increase

This can also be worked as many stitches into the work as may be required, but is similarly normally worked two or three stitches in.

Bring forward to working position one needle. Working with a two or three pronged tool, transfer the end stitches to the outside.

With a single end tool, pick up the loop from the third or fourth stitch and place it onto the empty needle.

Multiple stitch increase

When a pattern calls for more than two stitches to be increased at the left or right, use the closed edge cast on method as shown in the cast on by hand section, or use the chain method.

On the opposite side to the carriage bring forward into holding position the number of needles required. Using a spare piece of MY and the latch tool/tappet, work a chain stitch over each needle, working from the edge of the work to the outside.

Bring the same needles into holding position before knitting the next few rows.

Working with nylon cord

Use nylon cord when knitting a shaped neck and the pattern says knit back on nylon cord.

Bring the required number of needles into holding position and lay the nylon cord across them, making sure that the cord is in front of the latches.

Manually knit one needle at a time back into non working position.

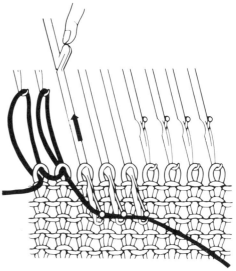

To replace the stitches onto the needles, with both hands pull both ends of the cord.

When all the needles are in working position hold one end of the cord and pull the other end upwards to unravel the stitches.

Cast off with latch tool

Before working cast off row *always* knit one row at the largest tension possible. When working with fine yarns, knit one row with the tension 3 or 4 numbers higher than the main knitting.

Bring all needles into holding position. On the side opposite to the carriage, hook the latch tool into the first stitch and push the stitch behind the latch. Hook the tool into the second stitch leaving this stitch in the hook. Bring the latch tool forward drawing the first stitch over the second.

Push the second stitch behind the latch. Hook the latch tool into the third stitch and repeat as before.

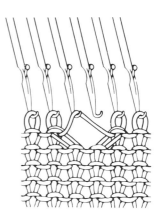

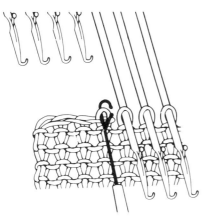

Then pick up the loop previously removed and place it onto the needle above where the bar was picked up from. Continue to knit.

To finish off pull the yarn through the last stitch with the latch tool.

Buttonholes

Small buttonholes are worked by transferring one stitch onto an adjacent needle, leaving the empty needle in working position.

This method works just as well when working on a single bed or double bed machine. When working with a double bed machine transfer the stitch from the front bed to the adjacent needle on the main bed—leaving the empty needle in working position.

Medium buttonholes

These are worked over two needles by transferring two stitches onto their respective adjacent needles leaving the empty needles in working position, then knitting one row.

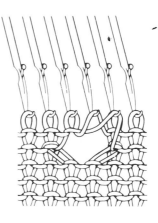

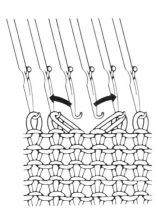

Remove the loop from the right stitch and pick up the bar beneath the stitch to the right. Knit one row.

Large buttonholes

These are worked over three or more stitches for any size of button.

Have a piece of MY ready to cast on the stitches at the top of the buttonhole.

Transfer one stitch onto the adjacent needle to the right and then transfer these two stitches onto the empty needle.

Bring the needle forward until the stitch at the back passes over the latch hook. Take the needle back, drawing the back stitch over the front one.

Continue to work, repeating all the above over the number of stitches required.

Place the last stitch onto the next needle on the left.

For the upper edge, cast on with MY using the chain method. Bring all the needles used for the buttonholes into holding position before knitting the next few rows.

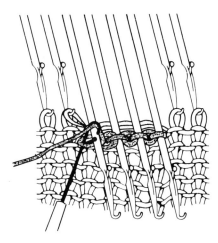

Finishing

Try to press knitwear on a large flat surface. First pin out each piece of knitting with the wrong side facing you, carefully checking the size.

After reading the manufacturer's or pattern instructions, press the knitting with a smooth action. Do not wet press unless stated in the pattern.

Backstitch

After letting the knitting cool from pressing, pin the pieces together. For the sleeve and side seams, backstitch gives a very simple, firm seam. Using a wool needle with a rounded point, join the seam by working small running stitches which overlap.

Mattress stitch

For a really professional finish, mattress stitch is the neatest stitch for sewing up knitwear. It can, however, be more difficult as it is worked on the right side of the garment. Working with the right side of the garment in view does make matching stripes and patterns much easier.

Join the yarn to the fabric, insert the needle into two bars of the knitting, one complete stitch in. Then take the needle across to the other piece and pick up the two corresponding bars.

Repeat this, working down the seam, it is not necessary to keep pulling the yarn, several stitches can be worked before pulling the yarn to join the seam.

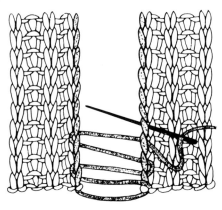

Grafting

When there are two open edges of the same length to be joined, graft stitch can be worked to produce a joining row which looks as if it has been knitted.

After pressing the pieces, working with a round ended needle threaded with the same yarn as the garment, lay the pieces together with the right sides facing.

Insert the needle from the back into the first stitch of the lower piece of knitting. Next, insert the needle from the back into the first stitch of the upper piece.

Insert the needle from the front, into the first stitch of the lower piece and into the back of the next stitch. Insert the needle from the front into the first stitch of the upper piece and into the back of the next stitch.

Continue to work the seam until all the loops are joined. Do not pull the yarn too tight.

Crochet edge

To trim the edge of neckline bands and hems with crochet stitch, join the yarn to the knitting with a crochet hook.

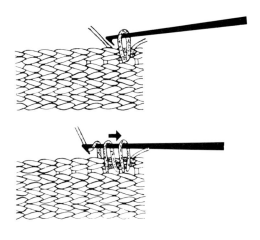

Work along the edge as shown.

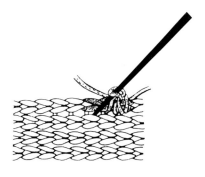

Continue to work along the edge, repeating these steps. At appropriate intervals, miss out a stitch from the knitting to form a firm edge.

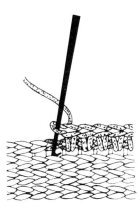

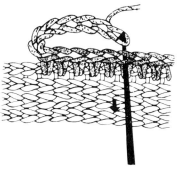

Continue to work in crochet stitch along the edge of the knitted fabric until the next buttonhole is required.

Continue to work in crochet stitch along the edge of the knitted fabric until the next buttonhole is required.

Crochet button loop

Working with a crochet hook, work crochet stitches as shown for making a crochet edge along the edge of the knitted fabric, up to the point where a buttonhole needs to be worked. Then crochet a chain to form a loop big enough to fit the size of button required. Remove the hook from the last chain stitch and insert it into the crochet stitch.

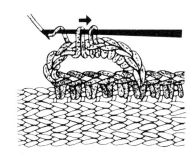

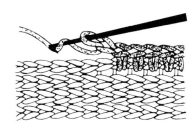

Pick up the last chain stitch and pull it through the crochet stitch. Then work crochet stitches along the chain stitches, working at least three more stitches than those worked in chain stitch.

ABBREVIATIONS

alt	Alternate	ins	Inch/es	r/s	Row/s
approx	Approximate	inc	Increase	rel	Release
beg	Beginning	K	Knit	rem	Remaining
carr	Carriage	mach	Machine	rep	Repeat
cms	Centimetre/s	M/bed	Main bed	rev	Reversing
cent	Centre	MT	Main Tension	st/s	Stitch/es
c.on	Cast on	MT − 1	Main Tension − 1	SS	Stocking Stitch
c.off	Cast off	MT + 1	Main Tension + 1	T	Tension dial
col(s)	Colours(s)	MY	Main Yarn	trans	Transfer
cont	Continue	n/s	Needle/s	WY	Waste yarn
dec	Decrease	NWP	Non Working Position	WP	Working Position
ev	Every	opp	Opposite		
FF	Fully Fashioned	patt	Pattern	*Note:*	Rib Tensions
foll	Following	pos	Position	T1/1	Tension 1 on both beds.
HP	Holding Position	RC	Row Counter	T10/8	Tension 10 on main bed
					Tension 8 on ribber bed.

Spring

Summer

9

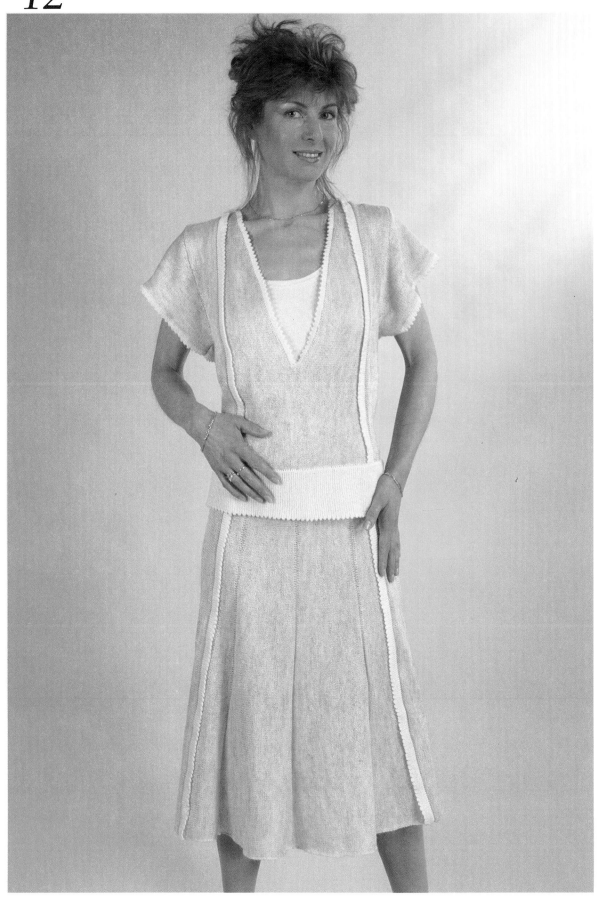

Autumn

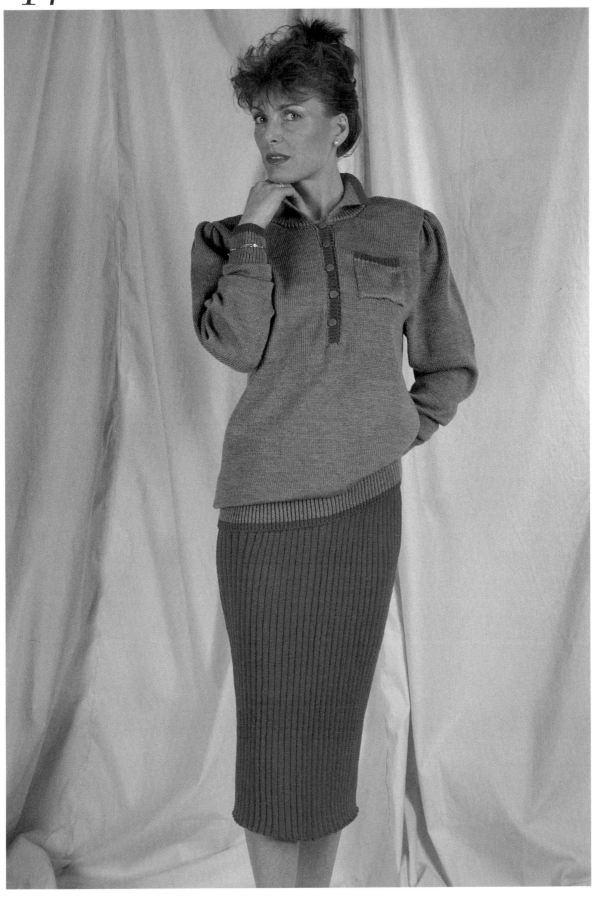

Winter

23

Evening

Spring

1

Pink
LONG SLEEVE SUIT

Sizes 34 (36 38 40 42) ins
(86 (91 97 102 107) cms) bust
36 (38 40 42 44) ins
(91 (97 102 107 112) cms) hip
Skirt length 29 ins (74 cms)

Materials 1 Cone Bramwell
Astrakan: Col A
250 gms matching Silky (2/30s
Acrylic Brights): Col A
200 gms Bramwell Astrakan: Col B
200 gms matching Silky (2/30s
Acrylic Brights): Col B
Elastic to fit waist

Tension 32 sts × 56 rs = 4 ins
(10 cms) using 1 end Poodle, 1 end
Silky
Tension dial approx 3

Note Purl side is right side of
garment

Skirt
C.on in WY 180 sts.
K few rs carr at left.
K 1 r with nylon cord.
RC 000, MT, both Cols A.
*Always taking yarn round last ns
in HP at opp end to carr, push 15
sts into HP next and foll alt rs. 4
times in all.
Push 10 sts into HP next and foll
alt rs. 11 times in all.
Push 10 sts at right back into WP
next and foll alt rs. 11 times in all.
Push 15 sts at right back into WP
next and foll alt rs. 4 times in all.
K 30 rs.*
Rep from * to * 13 (14 15 16 17)
times in all.

Pick up 1st row of knitting, MT,
K 1 r. T10, K 1 r.
C.off with latch tool.

WAISTBAND
(Knit two)
Bring forward 104 (112 120 128
136) ns.
Pick up sts from front or back
waist.
RC 000, MT, K 16 rs. T10, K 1 r.
MT, K 16 rs. C.off with latch tool.

TO MAKE UP
Steam press, sew waistband to
inside, thread elastic through waist.

Sweater
BACK
C.on in both Cols A, 1 x 1 rib, 143
(151 159 167 175) sts.
RC 000, T1/1, K 40 rs.
Both Cols B, K 6 rs. Both Cols A, K
4 rs.
Both Cols B, K 8 rs. Both Cols A, K
4 rs.
Both Cols B, K 10 rs. Both Cols A, K
4 rs.
Trans sts to M/bed. Inc 1 st.
RC 000, MT, K 10 rs.
Using both Cols B, K 4 rs. Both
Cols A, K 4 rs.

Both Cols B, K 12 rs.
Both Cols A, cont to K until RC 160.

Shape armhole at same time work stripe patt

**Both Cols B, K 4 rs. Both Cols A, K 4 rs.
Both Cols B, K 6 rs. Both Cols A, K 4 rs.
Both Cols B, K 8 rs. Both Cols A, K 4 rs.
Cont in both Cols B.**
C.off 5 (5 5 5 6) sts beg next 2 rs.
C.off 3 sts beg next 4 rs.
Dec 1 st both ends next and foll alt rs until 102 (108 120 132 140) sts.*
Cont to K until RC 262 (268 276 280 286).

Shape shoulders

C.off 5 (6 8 10 11) sts beg next 6 rs.
C.off 8 (8 8 8 6) sts beg next 2 rs.
Rel rem 56 sts on WY.

FRONT

K as for back to *.
Cont to K until RC 232 (238 246 250 256).

Shape neck

Push 59 (62 68 74 78) sts at left into HP, or K back onto nylon cord.
Always taking yarn round last ns in HP AT NECK EDGE, push 5 sts into HP next and foll alt r. K 1 r. Push 2 sts into HP next and foll alt rs 5 times in all.
K 16 rs. RC 262 (268 276 280 286).

Shape shoulders

C.off 5 (6 8 10 11) sts beg next and foll alt rs. 3 times in all.
C.off rem 8 (8 8 8 6) sts.
Take carr to left. Reset RC.
Work left side to match.
K 1 r across 56 sts.
Rel work onto WY.

SLEEVES

C. on in both Cols A, 1 x 1 rib, 63 (65 67 69 71) sts.
RC 000, T1/1, K 40 rs.
Trans sts to M/bed. Inc 1 st.
RC 000, MT, K 6 rs.
Inc 1 st both ends next and foll 6th rs until 120 (122 124 128 130) sts.
Cont to K until RC 196.

Shape top

Work stripe patt as for back ** to **.
AT SAME TIME

RC 000, c.off 5 (5 5 5 6) sts next 2 rs.
C.off 3 sts beg next 4 rs.
Dec 1 st both ends next and foll 3rd rs. 4 times in all.
Dec 1 st both ends next and foll alt rs. 30 (31 32 34 34) times in all until 38 sts rem.
RC 72 (74 76 80 80).
C.off 5 (3 3 3 2) sts beg next 2 rs.
C.off 0 (2 2 2 2) sts beg next 2 rs.
C.off 0 (0 0 0 2) sts beg next 2 rs.
C.off rem 32 sts.

COLLAR

C.on in both Cols A, 1 x 1 rib, 139 sts.
RC 000, T2/2, K 46 rs.

Trans sts to M/bed.
With K side facing, evenly pick up 28 sts cent front, 14 up shaping, 56 across back.
Push 41 sts at left into HP.
MT, K 1 r. T10, K 1 r.
C.off with latch tool.
Pick up 13 sts front shaping, 28 sts from cent front.
MT, K 1 r. T10, K 1 r.
C.off with latch tool.

TO MAKE UP

Join shoulder seams and then insert sleeves.
Sew side and sleeve seams.
Fold collar to outside.
Press with steam iron.

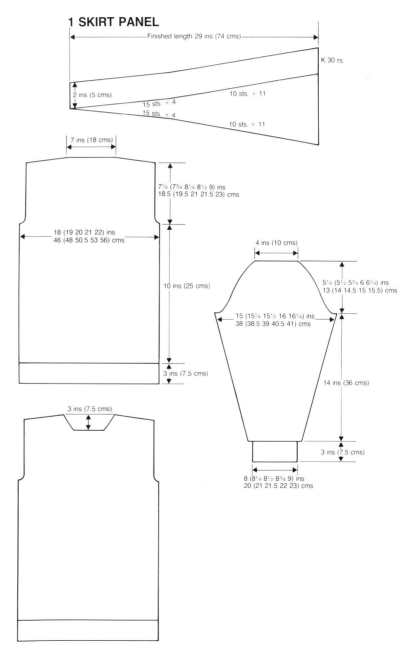

1 SKIRT PANEL

2

Denim Blue CARDIGAN SUIT

Sizes 32 (34 36 38 40) ins
(81 (86 91 97 102) cms) bust
34 (36 38 40 42) ins
(86 (91 97 102 107) cms) hip
Skirt length 31 ins (79 cms)

Materials 1 Cone Bramwell
Astrakan: Col A
300 gms Silky (2/30s Acrylic
Brights): Col B
Elastic to fit waist on skirt
Elastic to fit waist on vest top
White ribbon 5½ yds (5 m)
Card as shown
3 buttons

Tension 32 sts × 56 rs = 4 ins
(10 cms) using 1 end Astrakan
Tension dial approx 3

Note Purl side is right side of
garment

Skirt
Insert card and lock to K row 1.
C.on in WY 190 sts.
K several rs to hang weights onto.
Carr at left, K 1 r with nylon cord.
Leave card locked.
Col B, K 1 r. K 4 rs. Tuck. K 1 r.
Always taking yarn round last ns in
HP, Col A, bring 180 ns at left into
HP.
Push 10 sts at right back into WP
next and foll alt rs. 12 times in all.
Push 15 sts at right back into WP
next and foll alt rs. 4 times in all.
*RC 000, K 30 rs.
Col B, K 1 r. K 4 rs. Tuck. K 1 r.
Col A, bring 15 sts at left into HP
next and foll alt rs. 4 times in all.
Push 10 sts into HP next and foll
alt rs. 12 times in all.*
Col B, K 1 r. K 4 rs. Tuck. K 1 r.
Col A, bring 180 ns at left into HP.
Push 10 sts at right back into WP
next and foll alt rs. 12 times in all.

Push 15 sts into WP next and foll
alt rs. 4 times in all.**
RC 106.
Rep from * to ** 12 (13 14 15 16)
times.
Then rep from * to *.
Join seam.
Pick up first r of knitting.
MT, K 1 r. T10, K 1 r.
C.off with latch tool.

LINING
Work as for skirt, over 186 ns
omitting tuck rows.

WAISTBAND
Bring forward 104 (112 120 128
136) ns.
With knit side facing, pick up sts
from front or back of both skirt
and lining.
RC 000, MT, K 20 rs. T10, K 1 r.

MT, K 20 rs.
C.off with latch tool.

TO MAKE UP
Join waistband, fold to inside and
slip st into pos.
Thread elastic through waist.
Press.

Cardigan

FRONT
Insert card and lock to K row 1.
C.on in WY 150 sts.
K few rs ending with carr at left.
K 1 r with nylon cord.
Using 1 end Col A, MT, K 12 rs.
T7, K 1 r. MT, K 12 rs.
Turn up hem.
RC 000, MT, Col A, K 2 rs.

**Shape front and work pattern
At same time,**
work 60 rs shaping and stripe patt.

50

Always taking yarn round last ns in HP at left, push 5 sts into HP next and foll alt rs. 30 times in all.
Col A, K 14 (16 18 20 22) rs.
Leaving card in lock pos:
Col B, K 1 r. K 4 rs. Tuck. K 1 r.
Col A, K 34 (36 38 40 42) rs.
Col B, K 1 r. K 4 rs Tuck. K 1 r.

Front shoulder
Col A, K 34 (36 38 40 42) rs.
Col B, K 1 r. K 4 rs. Tuck. K 1 r.
Col A, K 15 (17 17 19 19) rs.
RC 117 (125 131 139 145).

Shape armhole
C.off 72 sts beg next r.
K 1 r. Mark right edge.
C.on 72 sts (e method) at left next r.
RC 120 (128 134 142 148).

Back shoulder
K 16 (16 18 18 20) rs.
*Col B, K 1 r. K 4 rs. Tuck. K 1 r.
Col A, K 34 (36 38 40 42) rs.*
Col B, K 1 r. K 2 rs. Tuck.
RC 179 (189 199 209 219).

Shape neck
Keeping patt correct from * to *,
Col B, dec 1 st at left next 3 rs.
Col A, dec 1 st at left next 5 rs.
Cont to K in patt until RC 291 (307 323 339 355).
Col A, inc 1 st at left next 5 rs.
Col B, inc 1 st at left next 3 rs.
RC 299 (315 331 347 363).

Back shoulder
Col B, K 2 rs. Tuck. K 1 r.
Col A, K 34 (36 38 40 42) rs.
Col B, K 1 r. K 4 rs. Tuck. K 1 r.
Col A, K 16 (16 18 18 20) rs.
RC 358 (376 396 414 434).

Shape armhole
K 1 r. C.off 72 sts beg next r.
Mark right edge.
C.on 72 sts (e method) next r.
RC 361 (379 399 417 437).

Front shoulder
Col A, K 15 (17 17 19 19) rs.
Col B, K 1 r. K 4 rs. Tuck. K 1 r.
Col A, K 34 (36 38 40 42) trs.

Shape front
Cont in patt, Col B, always taking yarn round last ns in HP, push 5 sts at left into HP next and foll alt rs. 30 times in all.
K 2 rs.
RC 478 (504 530 556 582).

FRONT BAND

MT, K 12 rs. T7, K 1 r. MT, K 12 rs.
Rel work on WY.

SLEEVES

(Knit Two)
C.on in WY 88 sts.
K few rs, carr at left.
K 1 r with nylon cord.
RC 000, MT, Col A, K 2 rs.
Make 5 holes.
*Trans cent, and 20th and 40th ns
both sides onto adjacent ns. K 6
rs.*
Rep * to * throughout, AT SAME
TIME K 6 rs.
RC 008.
Inc 1 st both ends next and foll 5th
rs until 162 sts.
Cont to K until RC 210.
C.off very loosely.

BACK WELT

Using Col B, 3 ends, c.on in 1 × 1
rib, 129 (135 143 151 159) sts.
RC 000, T0/0, using knit bar,
K 56 rs.
Trans sts to M/bed.
With K side facing, pick up sts
between markers on back.
MT, K 1 r. T10, K 1 r.
C.off with latch tool.

LEFT AND RIGHT FRONTS

Using Col B, 3 ends, c.on in 1 × 1
rib, 65 (71 75 79 83) sts.
RC 000, T0/0, using close knit bar,
K 56 rs.
Trans sts to M/bed.
With K side facing, pick up sts
from front (not front band).
MT, K 1 r. T10, K 1 r.
C.off with latch tool.

LEFT WELT BAND

Bring forward 40 ns.

With wrong side facing pick up sts
evenly along front welt.
RC 000, MT, Col A, K 12 rs. T10,
K 1 r.
MT, K 12 rs.
Rel work on WY.

Rep for right front working three
buttonholes on 7th and 18th rs.

CUFFS

Using Col B, 3 ends, c.on in 1 × 1
rib, 63 sts.
RC 000, T0/0, using close knit bar,
K 50 rs.
Trans sts to M/bed.
With wrong side facing, pick up sts
from sleeve.
MT, K 1 r. T10, K 1 r.
C.off with latch tool.

NECKBAND

Bring forward 60 (68 72 74 78) ns.
With wrong side facing, pick up sts
from back neck.
RC 000, MT, Col A, K 12 rs.
T7, K 1 r. MT, K 12 rs.
Rel work on WY.

TO MAKE UP

Join shoulder seams gathering $3\frac{3}{4}$
ins (9.5 cms) to 5 ins (12.5 cms).
Insert sleeves, gathering at top.
Join side and sleeve seams.
Join welts and bands.
Fold bands to inside and slip st
into pos.
Press.
Sew on buttons.
Thread white ribbon down sleeve
holes.
Give final press.

Vest Top

BACK AND FRONT ALIKE

C.on in WY 128 (136 144 152 160)
sts.

K few rs, carr at left.
K 1 r with nylon cord.
RC 000, Col A, MT, K 12 rs.
T7, K 1 r. MT, K 12 rs.
Turn up hem.
RC 000, MT, K 120 rs.

Shape armholes

C.off 5 sts beg next 2 rs.
C.off 4 sts beg next 2 rs.
C.off 3 sts beg next 2 rs.
Cont to K until RC 196.

Shape neck

Push 64 (68 72 76 80) sts at left
into HP.
Work on right side only.
Dec 1 st at neck next and foll alt
rs. 10 times in all.
K 14 rs.
RC 230.
C.off rem 20 (24 28 32 36) sts.

Work left side to match.
Rel cent sts on WY.
Join left shoulder seam.

NECKBAND

Bring forward 168 ns.
With wrong side facing, pick up sts
evenly from neck.
MT, K 1 r. MT − 1, K 5 rs.
T7, K 1 r. MT − 1, K 6 rs.
T10, K 1 r. C.off with latch tool.

ARMBANDS

Join shoulder seam.
Bring forward 130 ns.
With wrong side facing, pick up sts
around armhole.
RC 000, MT, K 1 r. MT − 1, K 5 rs.
T7, K 1 r. MT − 1, K 6 rs.
T10, K 1 r. C.off with latch tool.

TO MAKE UP

Join side seams, allow bands to roll
to right side.
Thread elastic through waist.

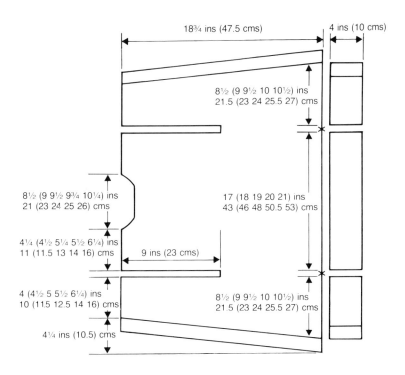

18¾ ins (47.5 cms)

4 ins (10 cms)

8½ (9 9½ 10 10½) ins
21.5 (23 24 25.5 27) cms

8½ (9 9½ 9¾ 10¼) ins
21 (23 24 25 26) cms

17 (18 19 20 21) ins
43 (46 48 50.5 53) cms

4¼ (4½ 5¼ 5½ 6¼) ins
11 (11.5 13 14 16) cms

9 ins (23 cms)

4 (4½ 5 5½ 6¼) ins
10 (11.5 12.5 14 16) cms

8½ (9 9½ 10 10½) ins
21.5 (23 24 25.5 27) cms

4¼ ins (10.5) cms

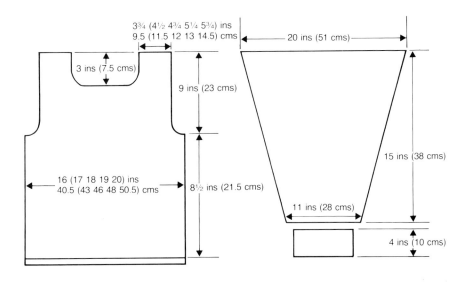

3¾ (4½ 4¾ 5¼ 5¾) ins
9.5 (11.5 12 13 14.5) cms

3 ins (7.5 cms)

9 ins (23 cms)

16 (17 18 19 20) ins
40.5 (43 46 48 50.5) cms

8½ ins (21.5 cms)

20 ins (51 cms)

15 ins (38 cms)

11 ins (28 cms)

4 ins (10 cms)

1 SKIRT PANEL

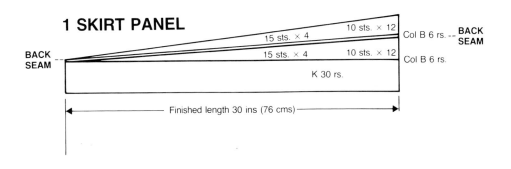

10 sts. × 12

15 sts. × 4

Col B 6 rs. --- BACK
SEAM

BACK
SEAM

15 sts. × 4

10 sts. × 12

Col B 6 rs.

K 30 rs.

Finished length 30 ins (76 cms)

3

Black-White
FAIRISLE
JACKET SUIT

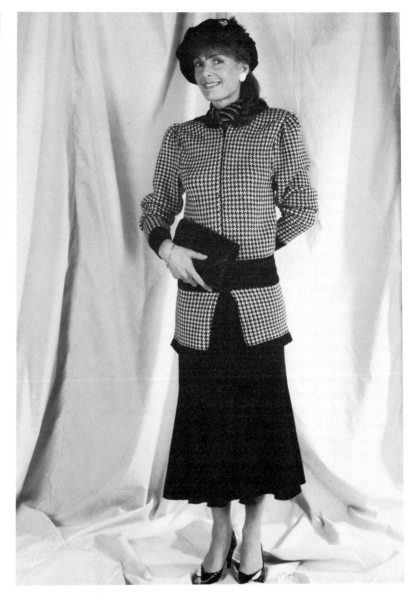

Sizes 32 (34 36 38 40) ins
(81 (86 91 97 102) cms) bust
34 (36 38 40 42) ins
(86 (91 97 102 107) cms) hip
Skirt length 30 ins (76 cms)

Materials 2 Cones BK 4-ply
Superwash Wool: Col A
1 Cone BK 4-ply Superwash Wool:
Col B
Elastic to fit waist
20 ins (50 cms) zip
Card as shown

Tension 34 sts × 40 rs = 4 ins
(10 cms) over fairisle
30 sts × 38 rs = 4 ins (10 cms) over
stocking stitch
Tension dial approx 7

Skirt
C.on in WY, 195 sts.
K few rs, carr at left.
K 1 r with nylon cord.
Col A, MT, K 14 rs.
Push 125 ns at left into HP.
Always taking yarn round last ns in
HP at left, push 5 sts into HP next
and foll alt rs. 13 times in all.
Push 5 sts at right into WP next
and foll alt rs. 13 times in all.
*RC 000, MT, Col A, push 125 ns at
left into HP.
Always taking yarn round last ns in
HP at left push 5 sts into HP next
and foll alt rs. 13 times in all.
RC 26.
Push 5 sts at right back into WP
next and foll alt rs. 13 times in all.
RC 52.
K 28 (30 32 34 38) rs across all ns.
RC 80 (82 84 86 90).
Bring 125 ns at left into HP.
Push 5 sts at left into HP next and
foll alt rs. 13 times in all.

Push 5 sts at right back into WP
next and foll alt rs. 13 times in all.
RC 132 (134 136 138 142).*
K 28 (30 32 34 38) rs across all ns.
RC 160 (164 168 172 180).
Bring 125 ns at left into HP.
Push 5 sts at left into HP next and
foll alt rs. 13 times in all.
Push 5 sts at right back into WP
next and foll alt rs. 13 times in all.
RC 212 (216 220 224 232). **
Reset RC 000.
Work 4 more panels from * to **,
then from * to *.
K 14 (16 18 20 24) rs.

Join back seam
Pick up first row of knitting placing
sts over last knitted row.
MT, K 1 r. T10, K 1 r.
C.off with latch tool.

WAISTBAND
Bring forward 110 (118 128 136
146) ns.
With K side facing, pick up sts
from front or back waist.
MT, K 16 rs. T10, K 1 r.
MT, K 16 rs. T10, K 1 r.
C.off with latch tool.

TO MAKE UP
Join waistband and slip st to inside,
thread elastic through waist.
Steam press.

Jacket

BACK
Insert card and lock to K row 1.
Using 1 x 1 n arrangement, c.on in
WY, 135 (143 151 159 167) sts.
K few rs, carr at left.
K 1 r with nylon cord.

RC 000, T4, Col A, K 10 rs.
Bring alt ns into WP, MT, K 12 rs.
Turn up hem placing sts onto
alt ns.
RC 000, MT, rel card, working in
fairisle, K 60 rs.
Lock card. Remove Col B.
Trans sts to 1 x 1 rib.
Col A only, T1/2, K 36 rs.
Trans sts to M/bed.
Rel card and work in fairisle.
K 70 rs.
RC 166.

Shape armholes

C.off 5 sts beg next 2 rs.
C.off 3 sts beg next 2 rs.
Dec 1 st both ends next and foll
alt r until 115 (123 131 139
147) sts.
Cont to K until RC 246.

Shape neck

Note card row no.
Push 87 (91 95 99 103) sts at left
into HP or K back onto nylon cord.
Work on right side only, dec 1 st
at neck next 6 rs.
Cont to K until RC 256.

Shape shoulders

C.off 4 (4 6 7 8) sts beg next and
foll alt rs. 3 times in all. K 1 r.
C.off 4 (6 6 7 8) sts beg next r.
K 1 r.
C.off rem 6 (8 6 6 6) sts.
Leave cent 59 sts in HP.
Work left side to match.
Rel cent sts on WY.

RIGHT FRONT

Insert card and lock to K row 1.
Using 1 x 1 n arrangement, c.on in
WY, 67 (71 75 79 83) sts.
K few rs, carr at left.
K 1 r with nylon cord.
RC 000, T4, Col A, K 10 rs.
Bring alt ns into WP.
MT, K 12 rs.
Turn up hem, placing sts onto alt
ns.
RC 000, MT, working in fairisle, K
60 rs.
Lock card. Remove Col B.
Trans sts to 1 x 1 rib.
Col A only, K 36 rs.
Trans sts to M/bed.
Rel card and work in fairisle.
K 70 rs.
RC 166.

Shape armholes

C.off 5 sts beg next r. K 1 r.
C.off 3 sts beg next r. K 1 r.
Dec 1 st beg next and foll alt r

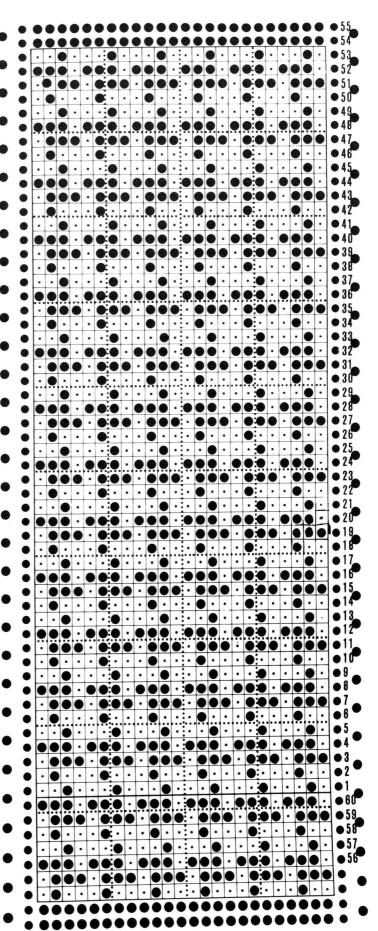

until 57 (61 65 69 73) sts rem.
Cont to K until RC 224.

Shape neck
Always taking yarn round last n
in HP push 20 sts at left into HP
next r.
K 1 r.
Push 1 st at left into HP next and
foll alt rs. 15 times in all.
22 (26 30 34 38) sts rem.
RC 256.

Shape shoulder
C.off 4 (4 6 7 8) sts beg next and
foll alt rs. 3 times in all.
K 1 r.
C.off 4 (6 6 7 8) sts beg next r.
K 1 r.
C.off rem 6 (8 6 6 6) sts.

Work left front to match
rev shaping.

SLEEVES
Col A, c.on in 1 x 1 rib 71 (73 75
77 79) sts.
RC 000, T1/1, K 40 rs.
Trans sts to M/bed. Inc 1 st.
RC 000, MT, rel card and work in
fairisle. K 4 rs.
Inc 1 st both ends next and foll 4th
(4th 4th 5th 5th) rs until 136 sts.
Cont to K until RC 150.

Shape top
C.off 5 sts beg next 2 rs.
C.off 3 sts beg next 2 rs.
Dec 1 st both ends next and foll
alt r until 116 sts.
RC 158.
Dec 1 st both ends next and foll
4th rs. 10 times in all until 96 sts.
RC 196.
C.off 2 sts beg next 10 rs.
C.off 4 sts beg next 10 rs.

C.off 6 sts beg next 2 rs.
24 sts rem.
RC 218.
C. off rem sts.

NECKBAND
Col A, c.on in 1 x 1 rib, 173 sts.
RC 000, T2/2, K 10 rs. T1/1, K 10 rs.
T0/0, K 9 rs.
T4/5, K 1 r.
Trans sts to M/bed.
With wrong side facing, pick up 35
sts held on WY at front, 8 sts up
front shaping, 87 sts across back, 8
sts down front, 35 sts held on WY.
MT, K 1 r. T10, K 1 r.
C.off with latch tool.

TO MAKE UP
Join shoulder seams.
Insert sleeves, sew in zip to fronts.
Press with steam iron, omitting
ribbed areas.

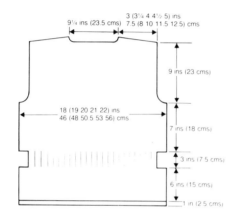

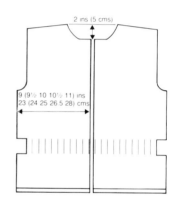

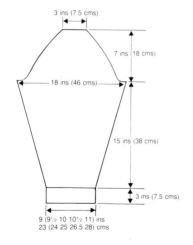

1 SKIRT PANEL

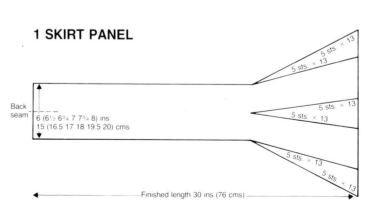

4

Royal-Blue RIB DRESS

Sizes 32/34 (36/38 40/42) ins
(81/86 (91/97 102/107) cms) bust
Length 44 ins (104 cms)

Materials 2 Cones DB
Matchmaker (2/3 ply)
18 ins (45 cms) zip
1 buckle

Tension 34 sts × 64 rs = 4 ins
(10 cms) over full n rib
Tension dials approx 1/2

FRONT
Using fine/close knit bar, c.on in
full n rib, 146 (162 178) sts.
RC 000, MT, K 4 rs.
Inc 1 st both ends next and foll
14th (14th 20th) rs, until 170 (186
196) sts.
RC 160 (160 166).
Mark both edges.
Cont to K until RC 320 (320 326).
Mark both edges. *
Dec 1 st both ends next and foll
4th (4th 5th) rs until 128 (144 162)
sts.
Cont to K until RC 416 (416 422).
Mark both edges.
Inc 1 st both ends next and foll 6th
rs until 144 (160 178) sts.
K 8 rs.
RC 496 (496 502).
Mark both edges. **
Cont to K until RC 616 (616 622).
Mark cent front.

Shape neck
Push 90 (98 107) sts at left into HP.
Work on right side only.
Dec 1 st at neck next and foll alt
rs. 17 times in all until 38 (46 55)
sts rem.
Cont to K until RC 656 (656 662).
C.off cent sts.

Shape shoulder
C.off 9 (11 13) sts beg next and foll
alt rs. 3 times in all.
K 1 r. C.off rem 11 (13 16) sts.
Work left side to match.

BACK
K as for front to *.
Dec 1 st at both ends next and foll
4th (4th 5th) rs until RC 368 (368
374).
DIVIDE WORK FOR BACK
OPENING.
Push all ns left of cent 0 into HP or
rel from mach on WY.
Cont to dec as before until 65 (73
82) sts.
Cont to K as for front to **.
Cont to K until RC 642 (642 648).

Shape neck
K 1 r. C.off 27 sts at cent beg

next r.
Dec 1 st at neck next 8 rs.
K 4 rs.
RC 656 (656 662).

Shape shoulder
C.off 9 (11 13) sts beg next and foll
alt rs. 3 times in all.
K 1 r. C.off rem 11 (13 16) sts.

Reset RC 368 (368 374).
Work left side to match.
for SHAPE NECK, omit 1 r and c.off
26 sts.

SLEEVES
Using fine/close knit bar, c.on in
full n rib 76 (84 94) sts.
RC 000, MT, K 6 rs.
Inc 1 st both ends next and foll 6th
(6th 7th) rs, until 170 sts.
Cont to K until RC 288.
C.off very loosely.

COLLAR

(Knit two)
Using fine/close knit bar, c.on in full n rib 81 sts.
RC 000, T2/3, K 10 rs.
T1/2, K 30 rs. T3/4, K 1 r.
C.off loosely.

BELT

C.on full n rib 12 sts.
RC 000, MT, K 340 rs.
C.off loosely.

TO MAKE UP

Join shoulder seams.
Insert sleeves between markers.
Sew side and sleeve seams joining at markers.
Sew collar to neckline.
Sew in zip.
Press lightly.

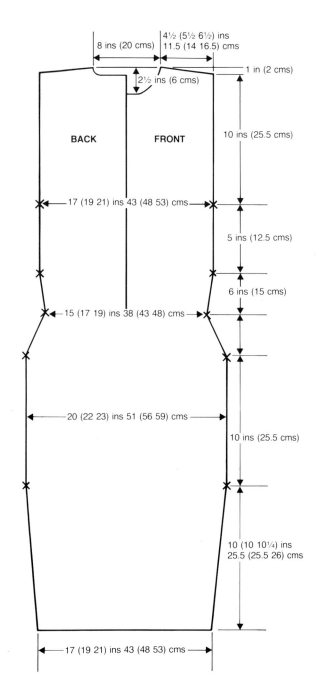

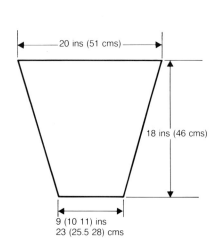

58

5

Royal-White
LONG LINE
JACKET SUIT

Sizes 32 (34 36 38 40 42) ins
(81 (86 91 97 102 107) cms) bust
34 (36 38 40 42 44) ins
(86 (91 97 102 107 112) cms) hip
Skirt length 30 ins (76 cms)

Materials 1 Cone Bramwell Duo
Spun 2 ply: Col A
100 gms Bramwell Duo Spun 2 ply:
Col B

Tension 31 sts × 49 rs = 4 ins
(10 cms) over full n rib
Tension dials approx 4/4

Skirt
(Knit two)
Col A, c.on in full n rib, 148 (156
164 172 180 188) sts.
Work c.on rs.
RC 000, MT, K 204 rs.
Mark both edges.
Dec 1 st both ends next and foll
5th rs until 100 (108 116 124 132
140) sts.
Cont to K until RC 330.
Mark both edges.
K 14 rs.
T8/8, K 1 r. MT, K 14 rs.
C.off loosely.

TO MAKE UP
Join side seams, fold waistband to
inside and slip st into pos.
Thread elastic through waist.
Press lightly.

Jacket

BACK
Col A, c.on in full rib, 140 (148 156
164 172 180) sts.
Work c.on rs.
RC 000, MT, K 200 rs.

Shape armholes
C.off 6 sts beg next 2 rs.
C.off 3 sts beg next 2 rs.

Dec 1 st both ends next and foll
alt r until 118 (126 134 140 148
156) sts.
Cont to K until RC 322.

Shape shoulders
C.off 7 (8 9 10 11 12) sts beg next
8 rs.
Rel cent sts on WY.

LEFT FRONT
Col A, c.on in full n rib, 70 (74 78
82 86 90) sts.
Work c.on rs.
RC 000, MT, K 30 rs.
Col B, K 4 rs.
Col A, K 6 rs. Col B, K 40 rs.
Col A, cont to K until RC 200.

Shape armhole
C.off 6 sts beg next r. K 1 r.
C.off 3 sts beg next r. K. 1 r.

Dec 1 st beg next and foll alt r.
59 (63 67 71 75 79) sts rem.
Cont to K until RC 292.

Shape neck
Push 16 sts at left into HP.
Push 1 st at left into HP next and
foll alt rs. 15 times in all until 28
(32 36 40 44 48) sts rem.
RC 322.

Shape shoulder
C.off 7 (8 9 10 11 12) sts beg next
and foll alt rs. 4 times in all.
Rel sts on WY.

RIGHT FRONT
K as for left front rev shaping.
Work stripes on RC 230.
Col B, K 4 rs. Col A, K 6 rs.
Col B, K 40 rs.
Cont in Col A as for left front.

SLEEVES

Col A, c.on in full n rib, 66 (70 74 78 82 86) sts.
Work c.on rs.
RC 000, MT, K 6 rs.
Inc 1 st both ends next and foll 6th rs until 130 sts.
Cont to K until RC 200.

Shape top

C.off 6 sts beg next 2 rs.
C.off 3 sts beg next 2 rs.
Dec 1 st both ends next and foll alt r.
K 1 r. 110 sts.
RC 208.
Dec 1 st both ends next and foll 4th rs. 10 times in all.

K 3 rs.
Dec 1 st both ends next and foll alt rs. 10 times in all until 70 sts rem.
RC 268.
C.off 3 sts beg next 18 rs.
C.off rem sts.

Work right sleeve

to match working stripes on RC 150.
Col B, K 4 rs. Col A, K 6 rs.
Col B, K 40 rs.
Cont in Col A, as for other sleeve.

NECKBAND

Col A, c.on in full n rib, 134 sts.
Work c.on rs.
RC 000, MT − 1/1, K 12 rs.

T8/8, K 1 r. MT − 1/1, K 11 rs.
T4/5, K 1 r.
Trans sts to M/bed.
With wrong side facing, pick up 31 sts held on WY, 5 sts up to shoulder, 62 sts held on WY, 5 sts up to shoulder, 31 sts held on WY.
MT + 2, K 1 r. T 10, K 1 r.
C.off with latch tool.

TO MAKE UP

Join shoulder seams, insert sleeves.
Sew side and sleeve seams.
Fold neckband to inside and slip st into pos.
Work 3 crochet buttonhole loops on right front.
Sew on buttons.
Press lightly.

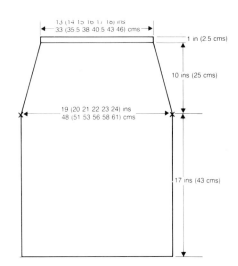

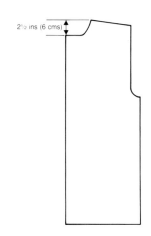

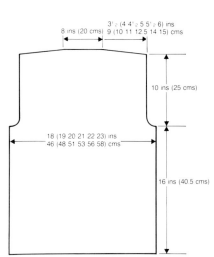

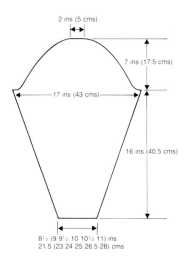

6

Green- White BATWING SUIT

Sizes 32/34 (36/38 40/42) ins (81/86 (91/97 102/107) cms) bust 34 (36 38 40 42 44) ins (86 (91 97 102 107 112) cms) hip Skirt length 30 ins (76 cms)

Materials 1 (2 2) Cones DB Colourscope 4 ply: Col A 1 cone DB Colourscope 4 ply: Col B

Tension 32 sts × 44 rs = 4 ins (10 cms) Tension dial approx 6

Skirt

C.on in WY 195 sts (97–0–98).
K few rs, carr at left.
K 1 r with nylon cord.
Always taking yarn round last ns in HP, K 6 rs.
RC 000, MT, Col A.
Bring 15 ns at left into HP next and foll alt rs. 7 times in all.
Push 10 sts into HP next and foll alt rs. 8 times in all.
Push 10 sts at right back into WP next and foll alt rs. 8 times in all.
Push 15 sts back into WP next and foll alt rs. 7 times in all.
K 14 rs. Push 115 sts at left into HP.
Col B, push 5 sts at left into HP next and foll alt rs. 15 times in all.
Push 5 sts at right back into WP next and foll alt rs. 15 times in all.
K 14 rs across all ns.
Push 15 sts at left into HP next and foll alt rs. 7 times in all.
Push 10 sts into HP next and foll alt rs. 8 times in all.
Push 10 sts at right back into WP next and foll alt rs. 8 times in all.
Push 15 sts back into WP next and foll alt rs. 7 times in all.*
RC 168.

Rep from * to *. 10 (11 12 13 14 15) times in all.
K 6 rs.
Rel work from mach on WY.
Graft back seam.

WAISTBAND

Bring forward 112 (116 120 124 128 132) ns.
With purl side facing, pick up sts from front or back waist.
MT-1, K 16 rs. T8, K 1 r.
MT-1, K 16 rs.
C.off with latch tool.

TO MAKE UP

Fold waistband to inside and sew into pos.
Thread elastic through waist. Press with warm iron.

Batwing top

BACK
Counting from 72nd (74th 76th) n left cent 0, c.on in WY 48 (52 56) sts.
K few rs, carr at left.
K 1 r with nylon cord.
RC 000, MT, Col B, K 2 rs.
Inc 1 st at right, next and foll alt rs. 80 times in all. K 2 rs.
C.on 16 sts at right (e method).
RC 164, 144 (148 152) sts.
Mark both edges.
Col A, K 12 rs. Col B, K 44 (54 66) rs.
RC 220 (230 242).*

Shape neck

Dec. 1 st at right next 7 rs.
K 11 rs.
RC 238 (248 260).

Col A, K 52 rs. Col B, K 11 rs.
Inc 1 st at right next 7 rs.
RC 308 (318 330).**
K 44 (54 66) rs.
Col A, K 12 rs.
C.off 16 sts at right.
44 (52 56) sts
Col B, K 2 rs.
Dec 1 st at right next and foll alt
rs. 80 times in all.
K 2 rs.
RC 528 (548 572).
Rel work on WY.

FRONT

K as for back to *

Shape neck

C.off 10 sts at beg next r. K 1 r.
C.off 5 sts beg next and foll alt r. K
1 r.
C.off 3 sts beg next and foll alt rs.
3 times in all. K 1 r.
Dec 1 st at right next and foll alt
rs. 3 times in all. K 1 r.
112 (116 120) sts.

RC 238 (248 260).
Col A, K 52 rs. Col B, inc 1 st at
right next and foll alt rs. 3 times in
all. K 1 r.
C.on 3 sts beg next and foll alt rs.
3 times in all. K 1 r.
C.on 5 sts beg next and foll alt r. K
1 r.
C.on 10 sts beg next r.
RC 308 (318 330).
Cont to K as for back from ** to
end.

WELTS

Col B, c.on in 1 x 1 rib, 135 (143
151) sts.
RC 000, T1/0, K 40 rs.
Trans sts to M/bed.
With wrong side facing, pick up sts
evenly from front or back waist.
MT, k 1 r. T10, K 1 r.
C.off with latch tool.

CUFFS

Col B, c.on in 1 x 1 rib, 65 (69 71)

sts.
RC 000, T1/0, K 40 rs.
Trans sts to M/bed.
With wrong side facing, pick up sts
evenly from sleeve edge.
MT, K 1 r. T10, K 1 r.
C.off with latch tool.
Join 1 shoulder to marker.

NECKBAND

Col B, c.on in 1 x 1 rib, 161 sts.
RC 000, T1/1, K 10 rs. T0/0, K 10 rs.
T8/8, K 1 r. T0/0, K 10 rs.
T1/1, K 9 rs. T4/3, K 1 r.
Trans sts to M/bed.
With wrong side facing, pick up sts
evenly around neck. MT, K 1 r.
T10, K 1 r. C.off with latch tool.

TO MAKE UP

Join upper sleeve seams.
Sew under sleeve and side seams.
Fold neckband to inside and slip st
into pos. Press.

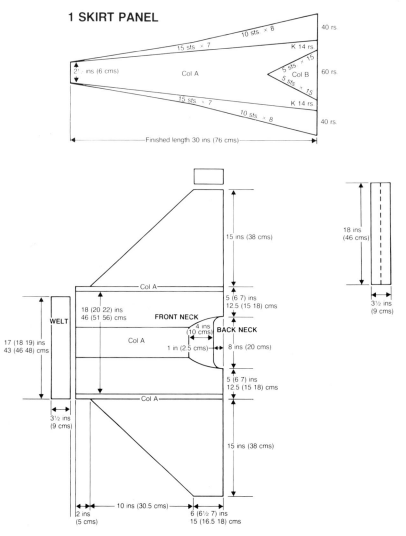

1 SKIRT PANEL

Summer

7

Turquoise
SHORT SLEEVE SUIT

Sizes 34 (36 38 40 42 44) ins
(86 (91 97 102 107 112) cms) bust
36 (38 40 42 44 46) ins
(91 (97 102 107 112 117) cms) hip
Skirt length 29 ins (74 cms)

Materials 1 Cone Bramwell
Astrakan: Col A
250 gms matching Silky (2/30s
Acrylic Brights): Col A
200 gms Bramwell Astrakan: Col B
200 gms matching Silky (2/30s
Acrylic Brights): Col B
Elastic to fit waist

Tension 32 sts × 56 rs = 4 ins
(10 cms) using 1 end both yarns
Col A
Tension dial approx 3

Note Purl side is right side of
garment

Skirt

C.on in WY 190 sts.
K few rs, carr at left.
K 1 r with nylon cord.
Using both ends Col B, MT, K 2 rs.
Bring 170 sts at left into HP.
Both ends Col A, push 10 sts at
right back into WP next and foll alt
rs. 12 times in all.
Push 15 sts at right back into WP
next and foll alt rs. 4 times in all.
K 30 rs.
*Push 15 sts at left in HP next and
foll alt rs. 4 times in all.
Push 10 sts at left into HP next and
foll alt rs. 12 times in all.*

Col B, K 2 rs across all ns.
Bring 170 ns back into HP.
Col A, push 10 sts at right back
into WP next and foll alt rs. 12
times in all.
Push 15 sts at right back into WP
next and foll alt rs. 4 times in all.
K 30 rs.**
Rep from * to ** 13 (14 15 16 17
18) times in all then from * to *
once.
Join back seam.
Pick up first row of knitting, MT, K
1 r. T10, K 1 r.
C.off with latch tool.

WAISTBAND
(Knit two)
Bring forward 104 (112 120 128 136
144) ns.
With K side facing, pick up sts
from front or back waist.
Both ends Col A, MT, K 16 rs. T10,
K 1 r.
MT, K 16 rs. T10, K 1 r.
C.off with latch tool.
TO MAKE UP
Join waistband, fold to inside and
slip stitch into pos.
Thread elastic through waist.
Steam press.

Sweater

BACK

C.on in Col A 143 (151 159 167 175 183) sts.
RC 000, T1/1, K 15 rs.
Col B, K 2 rs. Col A, K 4 rs.
Col B, K 4 rs. Col A, K 4 rs.
Col B, K 6 rs. Col A, K 7 rs. RC 42.
Trans sts to M/bed. Inc 1 st.
RC 000, MT, K 120 rs.
Work stripe patt.
Col B, K 2 rs. Col A, K 4 rs.
Col B, K 4 rs. Col A, K 4 rs.
Col B, K 6 rs. Col A, K 4 rs.
Col B, K 8 rs. Col A, K 4 rs.
Cont in Col B. RC 156.

Shape armhole

C.off 5 (5 5 5 6 8) sts beg next 2 rs.
C.off 3 sts beg next 4 rs.
Dec 1 st both ends next and foll alt rs until 102 (108 120 132 140 144) sts rem.*
Cont to K until RC 258 (264 272 276 282 282).

Shape shoulders

C.off 5 (6 8 10 11 11) sts beg next 6 rs.
C.off 8 (8 8 8 9 11) sts beg next 2 rs.
Rel rem 56 sts on WY.

FRONT

K as for Back to *.
Cont to K until RC 228 (234 242 246 252 252).

Shape neck

Push 59 (62 68 74 78 80) sts at left into HP or K back onto nylon cord.
Always taking yarn round last ns in HP at cent, push 5 sts into HP next and foll alt rs. 4 times in all.
Cont to K until RC 258 (264 272 276 282 282).

Shape shoulder

C.off 5 (6 8 10 11 11) sts beg next and foll alt rs. 3 times in all.
C.off rem 8 (8 8 8 9 11) sts.
Work left side to match.
K 1 r across 56 sts in HP.
Rel on WY.

SLEEVES

C.on in both Cols A 95 (99 103 107 111 115) sts.
RC 000, T1/1, K 18 rs.
Trans sts to M/bed. Inc 1 st.
RC 000, MT, K 2 rs.
Inc 1 st both ends next and foll alt rs until 108 (116 120 124 128 128) sts.

On RC 50, work stripe patt as for back.
Cont to K until RC 86.
Cont in Col B.

Shape top

C.off 5 (5 5 5 6 6) sts beg next 2 rs.
C.off 3 sts beg next 4 rs.
Dec 1 st both ends next and foll alt rs until 44 (50 52 52 52 52) sts rem.
C.off 3 (3 3 2 2 2) sts beg next 4 (6 6 6 6 6) rs.
C.off rem 32 (32 34 40 40 40) sts.

COLLAR

C.on in both Cols A 131 sts.
RC 000, T2/3, K 7 rs.

Col B, K 2 rs. Col A, K 4 rs.
Col B, K 4 rs. Col A, K 4 rs.
Col B, K 6 rs. Col A, K 15 rs.
Trans sts to M/bed. RC 42.
Working from cent front to cent back, with K side facing, pick up sts evenly around ½ of neck.
Push all ns left into HP.
MT, K 1 r. T10, K 1 r.
C.off with latch tool.
Rep * to * for left side.

TO MAKE UP

Join shoulder seams, insert sleeves, sew side and sleeve seams, fold collar to outside.
Steam press.

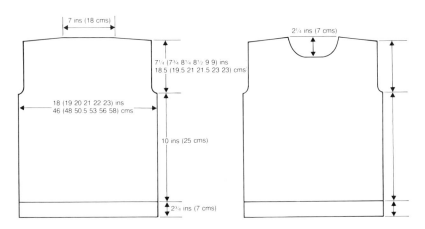

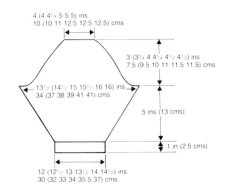

1 SKIRT PANEL

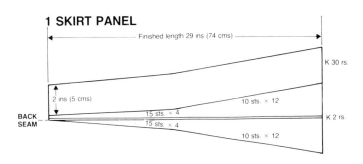

8

Lemon
SHORT SLEEVE SUIT

Sizes 32 (34 36 38 40) ins
(81 (86 91 97 102) cms) bust
34 (36 38 40 42) ins
(86 (91 97 102 107) cms) hip
Skirt length 31 ins (79 cms)

Materials
1 Cone Bramwell Astrakan: Col A
250 gms Silky (2/30s Acrylic
Brights): Col B
Elastic to fit waist
Card as shown
3 ends Silky Col B for sweater

Tension 32 sts × 56 rs = 4 ins
(10 cms) using 1 end Col A
Tension dial approx 3

Note Purl side is right side of
garment

Skirt
Insert card and lock to K row 1.
C.on in WY 190 sts.
K several rs to hang weights onto.
Carr at left, K 1 r with nylon cord.
*Using 1 end Col B, leave card
locked, K 1 r to set ns.
K 4 rs. Tuck. K 1 r.
Col A, bring 180 ns at left into HP.
Always taking yarn round last ns in
HP, push 10 sts at right back into
WP next and foll alt rs. 12 times
in all.
Push 15 sts at right back into WP
next and foll alt rs. 4 times in all.
K 30 rs.
Push 15 sts at left into HP next and
foll alt rs. 4 times in all.
Push 10 sts at left into HP next and
foll alt rs. 12 times in all.**
Rep from * to ** 13 (14 15 16 17)
times in all.
Join back seam.
Bring all ns back to WP.
Pick up first row of knitting.
MT, K 1 r. T10, K 1 r.
C.off with latch tool.

LINING
Work as for skirt over 186 ns
omitting tuck rows.

WAISTBAND
Bring forward 104 (112 120 128
136) ns.
With knit side facing, pick up sts
from front or back waist from both
skirt and lining.
RC 000, MT, K 20 rs. T10, K 1 r.
MT, K 20 rs. C.off with latch tool.

TO MAKE UP
Join waistbands and sew to inside.
Thread elastic through waist.
Steam press.

Sweater

BACK
Insert card and lock to K row 1.
Using 3 ends Silky Col B, c.on in

1 × 1 rib, 143 (151 159 167 175) sts.
RC 000, T0/1, K 40 rs.
Trans sts to M/bed. Inc 1 st.
RC 000, MT*. Col A, K 30 rs.
Col B, K 1 r. K 4 rs. Tuck. K 1 r.*
Rep * to * throughout.
Cont to K in patt until RC 158.

Shape armholes
C.off 5 sts beg next 2 rs.
C.off 3 sts beg next 4 rs.
Dec 1 st both ends next and foll
alt rs until 102 (108 120 132 140)
sts.*
Cont to K until RC 240 (248 258
264 272).

Shape shoulders
C.off 7 (8 10 12 13) sts beg next 6 rs.
Rel cent 60 (60 60 60 62) sts on
WY.

FRONT

K as for back to *.
Cont to K until RC 210 (218 228 234 242).

Shape neck

Push 61 (64 70 76 79) sts at left into HP or K back onto nylon cord. Work on right side.
Always taking yarn round last ns in HP at neck edge, push 5 sts into HP next and foll alt r. K 1 r.
Push 2 sts into HP next and foll alt rs. 5 times in all.
Push 0 (0 0 0 1) st into HP next r.
Cont to K until RC 240 (248 258 264 272).

Shape shoulders

C.off 7 (8 10 12 13) sts beg next and foll alt rs. 3 times in all.
Take carr to left, reset RC.
Work left side to match.
K 1 r across cent 60 (60 60 60 62) ns.

Rel work on WY.

SLEEVES

C.on in Col B 95 (97 99 101 103) sts.
RC 000, T1/0, K 18 rs.
Trans sts to M/bed. Inc 1 st.

At same time working in pattern

K 6 rs.
Inc 1 st both ends next and foll 5th rs until 112 (114 116 118 120) sts
Cont to K until RC 50.

Shape top

RC 000, c.off 5 sts beg next 2 rs.
C.off 3 sts beg next 2 rs.
Dec 1 st both ends next and foll 3rd rs. 17 (20 23 26 29) times in all until 62 (58 54 50 48) sts rem. RC 53 (62 71 80 89). K 3 (2 3 0 1) rs.
Dec 1 st both ends next and foll alt rs. 16 times in all.
RC 88 (96 106 112 122).
C.off rem sts.

COLLAR

C.on in Col 8 B, 1 × 1 rib, 149 (149 149 149 151) sts.
RC 000, T1/2, K 10 rs.
T0/1, K 20 rs. T1/2, K 10 rs.
Trans sts to M/bed.
With K side facing, pick up 30 sts from cent front, 14 up shaping, 60 (60 60 60 62) from back.
Push 45 sts at left into HP.
MT, K 1 r. T10, K 1 r.
C.off with latch tool.
Pick up 15 sts down shaping, 30 sts across front to cent.
MT, K 1 r. T10, K 1 r.
C.off with latch tool.

TO MAKE UP

Join shoulder seams.
Insert sleeves, gathering at top.
Sew side and sleeve seams.
Fold collar to outside.
Press.

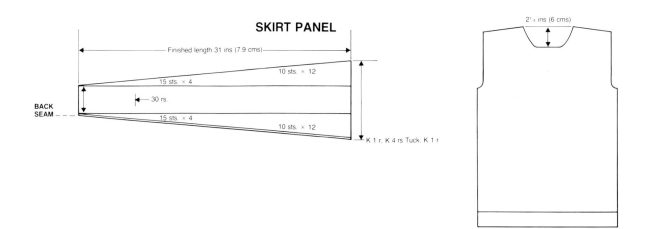

SKIRT PANEL

Finished length 31 ins (7.9 cms)

10 sts. × 12

15 sts. × 4

30 rs.

BACK SEAM

15 sts. × 4

10 sts. × 12

K 1 r, K 4 rs Tuck, K 1 r

2¼ ins (6 cms)

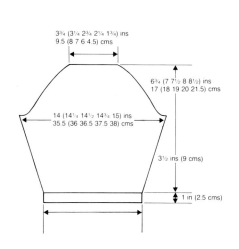

3¾ (3¼ 2¾ 2¼ 1¾) ins
9.5 (8 7 6 4.5) cms

6¾ (7 7½ 8 8½) ins
17 (18 19 20 21.5) cms

14 (14¼ 14½ 14¾ 15) ins
35.5 (36 36.5 37.5 38) cms

3½ ins (9 cms)

1 in (2.5 cms)

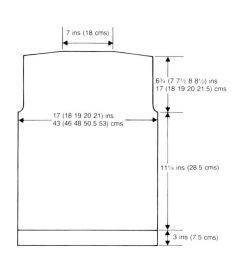

7 ins (18 cms)

6¾ (7 7½ 8 8½) ins
17 (18 19 20 21.5) cms

17 (18 19 20 21) ins
43 (46 48 50.5 53) cms

11¼ ins (28.5 cms)

3 ins (7.5 cms)

9
Mint-Green
SUMMER DRESS

Sizes 32 (34 36 38 40) ins
(81 (86 91 97 102) cms) bust
Length 43 ins (109 cms)

Materials 1 Cone Bramwell
Astrakan
Elastic to fit round arms
3¼ yds (3 m) white ribbon

Tension 32 sts × 56 rs = 4 ins
(10 cms) over ss
Tension dial approx 3

Note Purl side is right side of
garment

SKIRT
C.on in WY 195 sts.
K few rs, carr at left.
K 1 r with nylon cord.
Col A, MT, K 14 rs.
RC000, always taking yarn round
last ns in HP, push 15 sts at left
into HP next and foll alt rs. 4 times
in all.
Push 10 sts at left into HP next and
foll alt rs. 13 times in all.
Bring 190 ns at left into HP.
Push 10 sts at right into WP next
and foll alt rs. 13 times in all.
Push 15 sts back into WP next and
foll alt rs. 4 times in all.
K 30 rs.**
Rep * to ** 13 (14 15 16 17) times
in all.
K 16 rs.
Join back seam.
Pick up first row of knitting placing
sts over last row knitted.
MT, K 1 r. T10, K 1 r.
C.off with latch tool.

BODICE BACK
Bring forward 118 (126 134 146
156) ns.

With purl side facing, pick up 118
(126 134 146 156) sts from front or
back skirt.
RC 000, MT, K 10 rs.
Inc 1 st both ends next and foll
10th rs until 128 (136 144 152
160) sts.
Cont to K until RC 98.

Shape armhole
C.off 5 (5 6 8 8) sts beg next 2 rs.
Dec 1 st both ends next and foll
alt rs until 116 (120 124 128
136) sts.
Cont to K until RC 196.

Shape neck
Push 81 (83 85 87 91) sts at left
into HP, or K back onto nylon
cord.
Work on right side only.
Push 1 st at neck into HP next and

foll alt rs. 13 times in all until 22
(24 26 28 32) sts rem.
K 2 rs.
RC 224.

Shape shoulder
C.off 11 (12 13 14 16) sts beg next
and foll alt r.
Leave cent sts in HP.
Push 35 (37 39 41 45) sts at left
back into WP.
Work left side to match.
Rel cent sts on WY.

FRONT
K as for back working holes over
cent sts.
*Trans 11th–6th–1st sts left cent 0
and 2nd–7th–12 sts right cent 0
onto adjacent ns leaving empty ns
in WP
K 6 rs.*

Rep throughout.

SLEEVES

C.on in WY 96 (100 104 108 112) sts.
K few rs, carr at left.
K 1 r with nylon cord.
RC 000, MT − 1, K 8 rs.
MT + 3, K 1 r. MT − 1, K 8 rs.
Turn up hem.
MT, K 1 r.
RC 000, MT, K 4 rs.
Inc 1 st both ends next and foll 3rd rs until 120 (124 128 132 136) sts.
Cont to K until RC 40.

Shape top

C.off 5 (5 6 7 8) sts beg next 2 rs.

Dec 1 st both ends next and foll alt rs until 106 (110 112 114 116) sts.
K 4 rs.
RC 50.
Dec 1 st both ends next and foll 4th rs. 15 times in all.
K 3 rs.
C.off 2 sts beg next 14 rs.
C.off 0 (2 3 4 5) sts beg next 2 rs.
C.off rem 48 sts.
RC 124 (126 126 126 126).
Join shoulder seams.

NECKBAND

Bring forward 156 ns.
With K side facing, pick up sts evenly around neck.
RC 000, MT-1, K 8 rs.
MT + 3, K 1 r.
MT − 1, K 8 rs.
MT + 1, K 1 r.
C.off loosely.

TO MAKE UP

Insert sleeves, gathering at top.
Sew side and sleeve seams.
Fold neckband to inside and slip st into pos.
Steam press.
Thread elastic around sleeve edges.
Thread ribbon through lace holes at front.

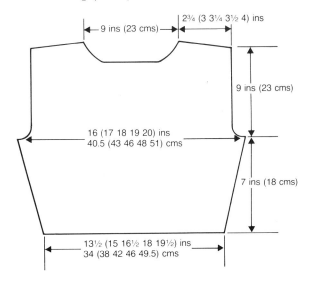

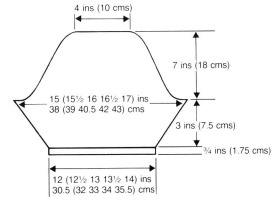

1 SKIRT PANEL

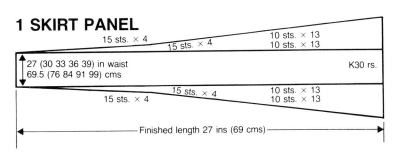

10
Peach-White
COLLARED DRESS

Sizes 32 (34 36 38 40 42) ins
81 (86 91 97 102 107) cms) bust
length 43 ins (109 cms)

Materials

1 Cone DB Colourscope 4 ply:
Col A
1 Cone DB Matchmaker 2/3 ply:
Col B
3 buttons

Tension 32 sts × 44 rs = 4 ins
(10cms) using Col A over ss
Tension dial approx 6

Note Purl side is right side of
garment

Skirt

C.on in WY 195 sts.
K few rs, carr at left.
K 1 r with nylon cord.
RC 000, MT, Col B, K 2 rs.
Always taking yarn round last ns in
HP, work HP shaping.
*Col A, bring 180 ns at right into
HP.
Push 15 sts at right back into WP
next and foll alt rs. 12 times in all.
K 22 rs.
Push 15 sts at left into HP next and
foll alt rs. 12 times in all. K 1 r.*
Col B, K 2 rs.**
Rep from * to **. 12 (13 14 15 16
17) times in all.
Then from * to * once.
Join back seam.
Pick up sts from first r of knitting
and place on corresponding ns.
MT, K 1 r. T10, K 1 r.
C.off.

BODICE BACK

Counting from cent 0 to left, c.on
in WY 72 sts.
K few rs, carr at left.
K 1 r with nylon cord.
*RC 000, Col A, MT, K 18 (22 24 26

28 32) rs.
AT RIGHT
C.on (e method) 64 sts.
136 sts, K 16 (18 22 24 28 30) rs.
Col B, K 6 rs. RC 40 (46 52 56 62
68).*

Shape neck

Col A, c.off 10 sts beg next r. K 1 r.
Dec 1 st at beg and foll alt rs. 6
times in all.
K 78 rs.
Inc 1 st beg next and foll alt rs. 6
times in all.
K 2 rs.
C.on 10 sts beg next r.
136 sts.
RC 146 (152 158 162 168 174).**
Col B, K 6 rs.
Col A, K 16 (18 22 24 28 30) rs.
C.off 64 sts beg next r.

K 17 (21 23 25 27 31) rs.
RC 186 (198 210 218 230 242).

BODICE FRONT

K as for back from * to *.

Shape neck

C.off 16 sts beg next r. K 1 r.
Dec 1 st at beg next and foll alt rs.
8 times in all. K 1 r.
K 30 rs.
C.off 40 sts beg next r. K 9 rs.
C.on 40 sts (e method) at right.
K 30 rs.
Inc 1 st at right next and foll alt rs.
8 times in all.
K 2 rs. C.on 16 sts at right
(e method).
RC 146 (152 158 162 168 174).
Cont to K as back from **.
C. off loosely.

Join shoulder seams.

ARMBANDS

Col B, c.on in 1 × 1 rib, 153 (157 161 165 169 173) sts.
RC 000, T0/0, K 8 rs. T 8/8, K 1 r.
T0/0, K 7 rs. T4/5, K 1 r.
Trans sts to M/bed.
With K side facing, pick up sts around armholes.
MT, K 1 r. T10, K 1 r.
C.off with latch tool.

BUTTONBAND

Bring forward 46 sts.
With K side facing, pick up sts from front opening.
RC 000, Col B, T3, K 12 rs.
T8, K 1 r. T3, K 12 rs.

C.off loosely.

BUTTONHOLE BAND

K as for buttonband, working 3 buttonholes on 7th and 19th rs on ns 5, 25 and 44 counting from right.

NECKBAND/COLLAR

Col B, c.on in full n rib, 171 sts.
*RC 000, T2/2, bring every 6th n on M/bed into HP, set lever on carr to HP.
K 4 rs. Set lever to K.
K 1 r.*
Rep from * to *. 3 times in all.
Insert close/fine knit bar.
T1/2, K 30 rs.
Trans sts to 1 × 1 rib, T0/0, K 6 rs.

Trans sts to M/bed.
*With knit side facing, pick up sts evenly from front band, front shaping to cent back.
Push rest sts to HP.
MT, K 1 r. T10, K 1 r.
C.off with latch tool.
Rep. from * for other side.

TO MAKE UP

Sew bodice side seam.
Join bodice to skirt.
Fold bands to inside and slip st into pos.
Join bands to cent front.
Sew on buttons.
Fold collar to outside.
Press.

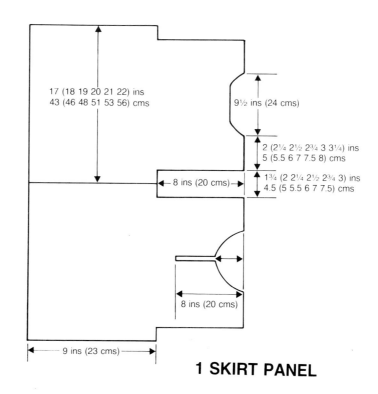

17 (18 19 20 21 22) ins
43 (46 48 51 53 56) cms

9½ ins (24 cms)

2 (2¼ 2½ 2¾ 3 3¼) ins
5 (5.5 6 7 7.5 8) cms

1¾ (2 2¼ 2½ 2¾ 3) ins
4.5 (5 5.5 6 7 7.5) cms

8 ins (20 cms)

8 ins (20 cms)

9 ins (23 cms)

1 SKIRT PANEL

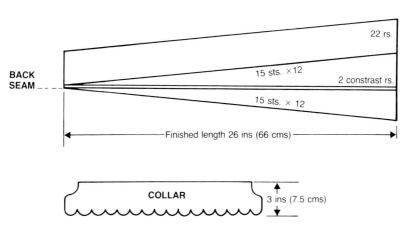

22 rs.

15 sts. ×12

2 constrast rs.

15 sts. × 12

BACK SEAM

Finished length 26 ins (66 cms)

COLLAR

3 ins (7.5 cms)

71

11 Blue-White PEPLUM CARDIGAN SUIT

Sizes 32 (34 36 38 40 42) ins
(81 (86 91 97 102 107) cms) bust
34 (36 38 40 42 44) ins
(86 (91 97 102 107 112) cms) hip
Skirt length 32 ins (81 cms)

Materials 2 Cones DB
Colourscope 4 ply: Col A
100 gms 2/30s Acrylic: Col B
Elastic to fit waist
6 buttons

Tension 32 sts × 44 rs = 4 ins
(10 cms) using Col A over ss patt
Tension dial approx 6

34 sts × 60 rs = 4 ins (10 cms)
using 2 ends Col B over full n rib
patt
Tension dials approx 3/1

Note Purl side is right side of
garment

Skirt

C.on in WY 195 sts.
K few rs, carr at left.
K 1 r with nylon cord.
RC 000, MT, Col B, K 2 rs.
Always taking yarn round last ns in
HP, work shaping.
* Col A, bring 180 ns at right into
HP.
Push 15 sts at right back into WP
next and foll alt rs. 12 times in all.
K 22 rs.
Push 15 sts at left into HP next and
foll alt rs. 12 times in all. K 1 r.*
Col B, K 2 rs. **
Rep from * to **. 13 (14 15 16 17
18) times in all. Then from * to *
once.
JOIN BACK SEAM
Pick up first r of knitting.
MT, K 1 r. T10, K 1 r.
C.off with latch tool.

WAISTBAND

Bring forward 106 (114 122 130 138

140) ns.
With K side facing, pick up sts
from front or back waist.
RC 000, MT, K 18 rs. T 10, K 1 r.
MT, K 18 rs. T 10, K 1 r.
C.off loosely.

TO MAKE UP

Fold waistband to inside and slip st
into pos.
Thread elastic through waist.
Press.

Jacket

BODICE

Counting from n 32 to the left of
cent 0, c.on in WY, 32 sts.
K few rs, carr at left.
K 1 r with nylon cord.
RC 000, MT, Col A, K 2 rs.
C.on 4 sts at right next and foll alt

rs. 24 times in all.
128 sts.
RC 50.
K 44 (50 54 60 66 72) rs.
C.off 64 sts beg next r.
MARK LEFT EDGE
K 1 r.
C.on (e method) 64 sts at right.
RC 96 (102 106 112 118 124).
K 44 (50 54 60 66 72) rs.
RC 140 (152 160 172 184 196).

Shape back neck

C.off 3 sts beg next r. K 1 r.
Dec 1 st at right next and foll alt
rs. 3 times in all. K 84 rs.
Inc 1 st at right next and foll alt rs.
3 times in all. K 2 rs.
C.on (e method) 3 sts at right.
RC 240 (252 260 272 284 296).
K 44 (50 54 60 66 72) rs.

C.off 64 sts beg next r.
MARK LEFT EDGE
C.on (e method) 64 sts at right.
K 44 (50 54 60 66 72) rs.

Shape front
C.off 4 sts beg next and foll alt rs.
24 times in all. K 2 rs.
32 sts.
RC 380 (404 420 444 468 492).
Rel work on WY.

BACK PEPLUM
Col A, c.on by hand, 135 (143 151
159 167 175) sts.
* RC 000, MT, K 54 rs.
Trans sts to 1 x 1 rib.
T0/1, K 24 rs.
Trans sts to M/bed. Inc 1 st.
With K side facing, pick up sts
from back between markers.
MT, K 1 r. T 10, K 1 r.
C.off with latch tool. *

FRONT PEPLUMS
(Knit two)
Col A, c.on by hand, 67 (71 75 79
83 87) sts.
Work as for back peplum from * to
*, picking up sts from front.

FRONT FRILLS
(Knit two)
Using 2 ends Col B, c.on in full n
rib, 193 sts.
* RC 000, T3/1, counting from 4th
n at right on M/bed, bring every
6th n into HP.
Set lever on carr to HP, K 4 rs.
Set lever on carr to K, K 1 r. *
Rep from * to *. 3 times in all.
K 10 rs. Trans sts to M/bed.
With K side facing, pick up sts
evenly from front to cent back.
Col A, MT, K 1 r. T10, K 1 r.
C.off with latch tool.

SLEEVES
Col A, c.on in 1 x 1 rib, 59 (63 67
71 75 79) sts.
RC 000, T1/0, K 36 rs.
Trans sts to M/bed. Inc 1 st.
RC 000, MT, K 10 rs.
Inc 1 st both ends next and foll 4th
rs until 104 sts.
Cont to K until RC 162.
T10, K 1 r.
C.off very loosely.

TO MAKE UP
Join shoulder seams, insert sleeves.
Sew side and sleeve seams. Join
neckband.
Sew on buttons (using last lacy
hole as buttonholes).
Work 2 rs double crochet around
bottom.
Sew on buttons.

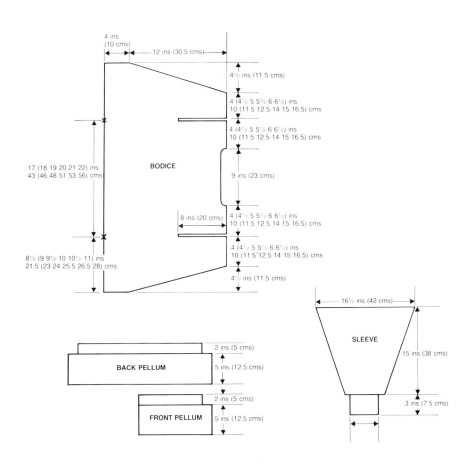

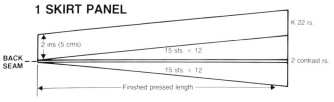

1 SKIRT PANEL

12

Pink
CAP SLEEVE
TOP SUIT

Sizes 32 (34 36 38 40 42) ins
(81 (86 91 97 102 107) cms) bust
34 (36 38 40 42 44) ins
(86 (91 97 102 107 112) cms) hip
Skirt length 30 ins (76 cm)

Materials 1 Cone DB Colourscope
4 ply: Col A
1 Cone DB Matchmaker 2/3 ply:
Col B
50 gms 2/30s Acrylic Brights: Col C
Elastic to fit waist

Tension 32 sts × 44 rs = 4 ins
(10 cms) using Col A
Tension dial approx 6

Note Purl side is right side of
garment

Skirt

CENTRE PANEL
C.on in WY 195 sts.
K few rs, carr at left.
K 1 r with nylon cord.
* Always taking yarn round last ns
in HP, RC 000, Col A, MT, push 15
sts at left into HP next and foll alt
rs. 3 times in all.
Push 10 sts at left into HP next and
foll alt rs. 14 times in all. K 16 rs.
Col C, K 2 rs across all ns.
Col A, K 16 rs.
Bring 185 ns at left back into HP.
Push 10 sts at right into WP next
and foll alt rs. 14 times in all.
Push 15 sts at left into WP next
and foll alt rs. 3 times in all.
RC 102. *
Rep from * to * 2 more times.
Rel work on WY.

SIDE AND BACK SKIRT
C.on in WY 195 sts.
K few rs, carr at left.
K 1 r with nylon cord.

RC 000, Col A, MT, work as for
cent panel from * to *. 5 (6 7 8 9
10) times in all.
Rel work on WY.

FRONT TRIM
(Knit two)
C.on in WY 195 sts.
K few rs, carr at left.
K 1 r with nylon cord.
RC 000, Col B, MT, K 10 rs.
Trans every other st onto adjacent
ns, leaving empty ns in WP.
T10, K 1 r. MT, K 10 rs.
Turn up hem.
Rel work on WY.
Bring forward 195 ns.
With purl side facing, pick up sts
from side of skirt.
Pick up sts from trim.
With K side of cent panel facing,

pick up sts.
Col A, MT, K 1 r. T10, K 1 r.
C.off loosely.
Rep for other side.

WAISTBAND
Press trims towards cent panel.
Bring forward 110 (120 130 140 160
170) ns.
With wrong side facing, pick up sts
from front or back waist.
RC 000, Col A, MT, K 16 rs.
T10, K 1 r. MT, K 16 rs. T10, K 1 r.
C.off loosely.

TO MAKE UP
Fold waistband to inside and slip st
into pos.
Thread elastic through waist.
Press.

Top

SIDE AND BACK BODICE

To the left of cent 0 c.on in WY 136 sts.
K few rs, carr at right.
K 1 r with nylon cord.
RC 000, Col A, MT, K 34 (38 44 50 56 60) rs.

ARMHOLE

C.off 64 sts at right beg next r.
Dec 1 st at right next 7 rs.
MARK LEFT EDGE
Inc 1 st at right next 7 rs. K 1 r.
C.on (e method) 64 sts at right.
RC 50 (54 60 66 72 76).
K 34 (38 44 50 56 60) rs.
RC 84 (92 104 116 128 136).

Shape neck

Dec 1 st at right next 8 rs.
K 88 rs.
Inc 1 st at right next 8 rs.
K 34 (38 44 50 56 60) rs.

ARMHOLE

C.off 64 sts at right beg next r.
Dec 1 st at right next 7 rs.
MARK LEFT EDGE
Inc 1 st at right next 7 rs. K 1 r.
C.on (e method) 64 sts at right.
RC 238 (250 268 286 304 316).
K 34 (38 44 50 56 60) rs.
RC 272 (288 312 336 360 376).
Rel work on WY.

FRONT PANEL

C.on in WY 136 sts.
K few rs, carr at right.
K 1 r with nylon cord.
RC 000, Col A, MT, K 10 rs.

Shape neck

Push 3 sts at right into HP next and foll alt rs. 18 times in all.
Push 6 sts at right into HP next and foll alt rs. 6 times in all.

RC 58.
Rel sts held in HP on WY.

C.on (e method) 6 sts at right next and foll alt rs. 6 times in all.
C.on 3 sts at right next and foll alt rs. 18 times in all.
K 10 rs.
RC 116.
Rel work on WY.

BODICE FRONT TRIMS

(Knit two)
C.on in WY 136 sts.
K few rs, carr at right.
K 1 r with nylon cord.
RC 000, Col B, MT, K 10 rs.
Trans every other st onto adjacent ns leaving empty ns in WP.
T10, K 1 r. MT, K 10 rs.
Turn up hem.
Rel work on WY.

Bring forward 136 ns.
With purl side of bodice facing, pick up sts from side, pick up sts from trim.
With K side of cent panel facing, pick up sts.
MT, K 1 r. T10, K 1 r.
C.off loosely.
Rep for other side.

NECK TRIM

C.on in WY 159 sts.
K few rs, carr at right.
K 1 r with nylon cord.
RC 000, MT − 1, Col B, K 6 rs.
Trans every other st onto adjacent ns leaving empty ns in WP.
T10, K 1 r. MT − 1, K 6 rs.
With K side of garment facing, pick up 69 sts from back and 90 sts held on WY from neck shaping.
MT, K 1 r. T10, K 1 r.
C.off with latch tools.

Second side: C.on 90 sts, work as for first side.

SLEEVES

C.on in WY 140 sts.
K few rs, carr at right.
K 1 r with nylon cord.
RC 000, Col B, MT − 1, K 6 rs.
T10, K 1 r. MT − 1, K 6 rs.
Turn up hem.
RC 000, Col A, MT, K 10 rs.
Always taking yarn round last ns in HP, at oppos end to carr:
Push 1 st into HP next 10 rs = 10 sts.
Push 2 sts into HP next 14 rs = 28 sts.
Push 3 sts into HP next 10 rs = 30 sts.
Push 4 sts into HP next 4 rs = 16 sts.
Push 5 sts into HP next 4 rs = 20 sts.
Push 6 sts into HP next 2 rs = 12 sts.
RC 54.
24 sts rem in WP.
Break yarn. Rejoin yarn at side.
K 2 rs across all ns.
C.off loosely.

BOTTOM WELT BAND

Press trims towards cent panel.
C.on in WY 136 (144 152 160 168 176).
K few rs, carr at right.
K 1 r with nylon cord.
RC 000, Col B, MT − 1, K 46 rs.
Trans every other st onto adjacent ns leaving empty ns in WP.
T10, K 1 r. MT − 1, K 46 rs.
Turn up hem.
With K side facing, pick up sts between markers from front or back waist.
MT, K 1 r. T10, K 1 r.
C.off with latch tool.

TO MAKE UP

Join shoulder seams, insert sleeves.
Sew side and sleeve seams, fold neckband to inside and slip st into pos. Join welts.
Press.

1 SKIRT PANEL

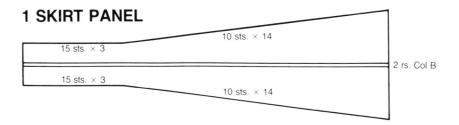

15 sts. × 3

10 sts. × 14

2 rs. Col B

15 sts. × 3

10 sts. × 14

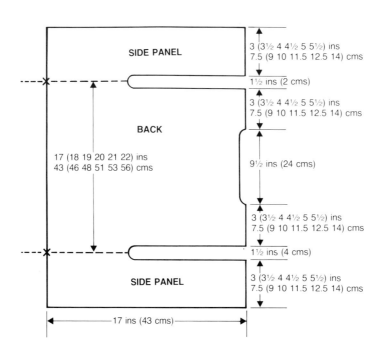

SIDE PANEL

3 (3½ 4 4½ 5 5½) ins
7.5 (9 10 11.5 12.5 14) cms

1½ ins (2 cms)

3 (3½ 4 4½ 5 5½) ins
7.5 (9 10 11.5 12.5 14) cms

BACK

9½ ins (24 cms)

17 (18 19 20 21 22) ins
43 (46 48 51 53 56) cms

3 (3½ 4 4½ 5 5½) ins
7.5 (9 10 11.5 12.5 14) cms

1½ ins (4 cms)

SIDE PANEL

3 (3½ 4 4½ 5 5½) ins
7.5 (9 10 11.5 12.5 14) cms

17 ins (43 cms)

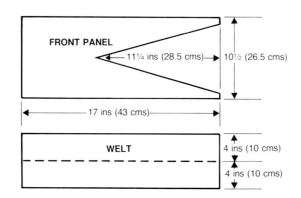

FRONT PANEL

11¼ ins (28.5 cms)

10½ (26.5 cms)

17 ins (43 cms)

WELT

4 ins (10 cms)

4 ins (10 cms)

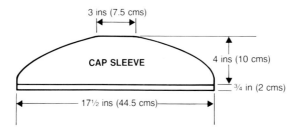

3 ins (7.5 cms)

CAP SLEEVE

4 ins (10 cms)

¾ in (2 cms)

17½ ins (44.5 cms)

Autumn

13

Rust-Brown
FAIRISLE
JACKET SUIT

Sizes 34 (36 38 40 42) ins
(86 (91 97 102 107) cms) bust
36 (38 40 42 44) ins
(91 (97 102 107 112) cms) hip
Skirt length 30 ins (76 cms)

Materials 3 Cones BK Superwash
Wool: Col A
1 cone BK Superwash Wool: Col B
Elastic to fit waist
6 cuff buttons
Card as shown
48 ins (122 cms) $\frac{3}{4}$ in (2 cms) wide
Vilene

Tension 36 sts × 40 rs = 4 ins (10
cms) over fairisle
Tension dial approx 7
30 sts × 38 rs = 4 ins (10 cms)
over ss
Tension dial approx 7

Note Purl side of skirt is right side
of garment.

Skirt
C.on in WY 195 sts.
K few rs, carr at left.
K 1 r with nylon cord.
Col A, MT, K 16 (18 20 22 24) rs.
Always taking yarn round last ns in
HP, push 125 sts at left into HP.
Push 5 sts at left into HP next and
foll alt rs. 13 times in all.
Push 5 sts at right into WP next
and foll alt rs. 13 times in all.
* RC 000, push 125 ns at left into
HP.
Always taking yarn round last n in
HP, at left push 5 sts into HP next
and foll alt rs. 13 times in all.
RC 26.

Push 5 sts at right back into WP
next and foll alt rs. 13 times in all.
RC 52.
K 34 (38 42 46 50) rs across all ns.
RC 86 (90 94 98 102).
Bring 125 ns at left into HP.
Push 5 sts at left into HP next and
foll alt rs. 13 times in all.
Push 5 sts at right back into WP
next and foll alt rs. 13 times in all.
RC 138 (142 146 150 154). **
K 34 (38 42 46 50) rs across all ns.
RC 172 (180 188 196 204).
Bring 125 ns at left into HP.
Push 5 sts at left into HP next and
foll alt rs. 13 times in all.

Push 5 sts at right back into WP
next and foll alt rs. 13 times in all. *
RC 224 (232 240 248 256).
Reset RC 000, work 4 more panels.
From * to * then from * to **.
K 18 (20 22 24 26) rs.
Join back seam.
Pick up first row of knitting placing
sts over last row knitting.
MT, K 1 r. T10, K 1 r.
C.off with latch tool.
WAISTBAND
Bring forward 118 (128 136 146
154) ns.
With knit side facing, pick up sts
evenly along front or back waist.

MT, K 16 rs. T10, K 1 r.
MT, K 16 rs. T10, K 1 r.
C.off with latch tool.

TO MAKE UP
Join waistband and slip st to inside.
Thread elastic through waist.
Work 2 rs double crochet around
hem.

Jacket

BACK
Insert card and lock to K row 1.
C.on in WY 162 (172 180 190
198) sts.
K few rs, carr at right.
K 1 r with nylon cord.
RC 000, MT, Col A, K 10 rs.
T10, K 1 r. MT, K 10 rs.
Turn up hem.
RC 000, MT, working in fairisle, K
112 rs.

Shape armhole
C.off 12 sts beg next 2 rs.
Cont to K until RC 202.

Shape neck
Mark card row no.
Push 106 (111 115 120 124) sts at
left into HP or K back onto nylon
cord.
Work on right side only.
Dec 1 st at neck next 8 rs.
K 2 rs.
RC 212.

Shape shoulder
C.off 8 (9 11 12 14) sts beg next
and foll alt r. K 1 r.
C.off rem 8 (11 11 14 14) sts.
Leave cent 74 sts in HP.
Work left side to match.
Rel cent sts on WY.

RIGHT FRONT
Insert card and lock to K row 1.
C.on in WY 74 (78 82 86 92) sts.
K few rs, carr at right.
K 1 r with nylon cord.
RC 000, MT, Col A, K 10 rs.
T10, K 1 r. MT, K 10 rs.
Turn up hem.
RC 000, MT, working in fairisle, K
112 rs.

Shape armhole
C.off 12 sts beg next r.
Cont to K until RC 180.

Shape neck
Push 23 (22 22 23 23) sts at left
into HP next r. K 1 r.
Push 1 st at neck into HP next and
foll alt rs. 15 times in all until 24

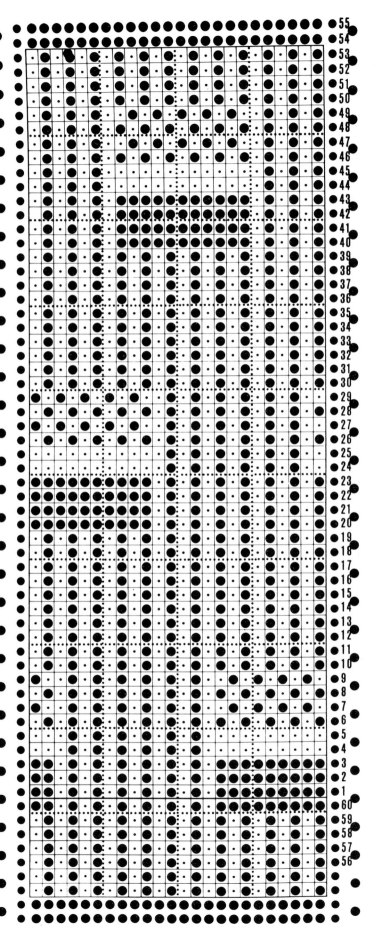

(29 33 38 42) sts rem.
RC 212.

Shape shoulder
C.off 8 (9 11 12 14) sts beg next and foll alt r. K 1 r.
C.off rem 8 (11 11 14 14) sts.
Work left to match, reversing shaping.
Join shoulder seams.

NECKBAND
Bring forward 161 ns.
With wrong side facing, pick up sts evenly around neck placing 2 sts on some ns.
RC 000, MT − 1, Col A, K 4 rs.
MT − 2, K 6 rs. T10, K 1 r.
MT − 2, K 6 rs. MT − 1, K 3 rs.
MT + 1, K 1 r. C.off loosely.

FRONT TRIMS
(Knit two)
Bring forward 198 ns.
With wrong side facing out fold armhole edge towards you.
Working on 11th row in from shoulder, pick up sts all down front.
RC 000, MT, Col A, K 8 rs.
T10, K 1 r. MT, K 7 rs.
C.off loosely.

FRONT BANDS
(Knit two)
Bring forward 172 ns.
With wrong side facing, pick up sts down front edge.
RC 000, MT, Col A, K 10 rs.
T10, K 1 r. MT, K 10 rs.
T10, K 1 r. C.off loosely.

SLEEVES
Insert card and lock to K row 1.
Counting from 6th n left cent 0, to the left, c.on in WY 42 (44 46 49 51) sts.
K few rs, carr at right.
K 1 r with nylon cord.
RC 000, MT, Col A, K 10 rs.
T10, K 1 r. MT, K 10 rs.
Turn up hem.
RC 000, MT, working in fairisle, K 24 rs.
MARK CARD ROW No.
Break off yarns.
Put all sts into HP.
Reset card to K row 1.
To the right of cent 0, leaving 5 empty ns in cent, c.on in WY 43 (45 47 50 53) sts.
K few rs, carr at right.
K 1 r with nylon cord.

RC 000, MT, Col A, K 10 rs.
T10, K 1 r. MT, K 10 rs.
Turn up hem.
RC 000, MT, working in fairisle, K 24 rs.
With spare piece of Col A, c.on by hand over cent 5 st (add weight).
90 (94 98 104 108) sts. Working in fairisle, inc 1 st both ends next and foll 3rd rs until 180 sts.
Cont to K until RC 169.
T10, K 1 r.
C.off loosely.

CUFF TRIMS
(Knit four)
Bring forward 29 ns.

With wrong side facing, pick up sts along sleeve opening.
RC 000, MT, Col A, K 6 rs.
T10, K 1 r. MT, K 6rs.
T10, K 1 r.
C. off loosely.

TO MAKE UP
Insert sleeves, sew side and sleeve seams.
Fold front bands and trims to inside and iron on Vilene in between, slip st into pos.
Fold cuff bands in half and slip st into position, sewing top edges to sleeve c.on sts.
Steam press.
Sew on cuff buttons through both trims.

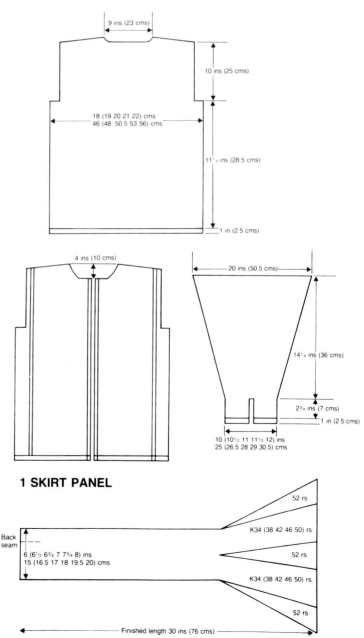

1 SKIRT PANEL

79

14

Grey-Heather
BUTTONED SWEATER SUIT

Sizes 34 (36 38 40 42) ins
(86 (91 97 102 107) cms) bust
36 (38 40 42 44) ins
(91 (97 102 107 112) cms) hip
Skirt length 29 ins (74 cms)

Materials 1 Cone Bramwell Lovat:
Col A
1 Cone Bramwell Pure Wool 4 ply:
Col B
5 buttons
Elastic to fit waist

Tension 30 sts × 42 rs = 4 ins
(10 cms) over ss
Tension dials approx 7

36 rs × 40 sts = 4 ins (10 cms)
over rib pattern
Tension dial approx 4/5

Needle arrangement:				
111	11111	11111	111	M/bed
11		11	11	Rib/bed

Skirt
(Knit 4 panels)
Col B, c.on in 1 × 1 rib, 120 (127
134 141 148) sts, working circular
c.on.
Trans sts to 5 × 2 rib (as diagram),
leaving 3 sts in WP at both ends
on M/bed to give ½ st each end for
seam.
RC 000, T4/5, K 270 rs.
Trans sts to M/bed.
K 1 r.
Rel work on WY.
Join panels leaving one open seam.

WAISTBAND
(Knit 2)
Bring forward 104 (112 120 128
136) ns.
With wrong side facing, gather 2

panels onto ns.
RC 000, MT − 1, K 16 rs.
T10, K 1 r. MT − 1, K 16 rs.
T10, K 1 r.
C.off loosely.

TO MAKE UP
Join last seam, fold waistband to
inside and slip st into pos.
Thread elastic through waist.
Press with steam iron.

Top

BACK
Col B, c.on in 1 × 1 rib, 127 (135
143 149 157) sts.
RC 000, T1/1, K 6 rs.
Col B, K 30 rs.
RC 36.
Trans sts to M/bed. Inc 1 st.
RC 000, MT, K 148 rs.

Shape armholes
C.off 6 sts beg next 2 rs.
C.off 3 sts beg next 2 rs.
Dec 1 st both ends next and foll r.
K 1 r.
106 (114 122 128 136) sts.
RC 156.
Cont to K until RC 232.

Shape neck
Push 72 (78 82 85 89) sts at left
into HP, or K back onto nylon
cord.
Work on right side only.
Dec 1 st at cent next 10 rs.

Shape shoulder
C.off 5 (6 7 8 9) sts beg next and
foll alt rs. 3 times in all.
K 1 r.
C.off rem 7 (8 9 9 10) sts.

Leave cent 42 sts in HP.
Return 32 (36 40 43 47) sts at left
to WP.
Work left side to match.
Rel cent sts on WY.

FRONT
K as for back until RC 116.
C.off cent 6 sts with spare piece
MY.
Push all ns at left into HP, or K
back onto nylon cord.
Work on right side only.
Cont to K until RC 148.

Shape armhole
C.off 6 sts beg next r. K 1 r.
C.off 3 sts beg next r. K 1 r.
Dec 1 st beg next and foll alt r.
K 1 r.
RC 156.
Cont to K until RC 212.

Shape neck
Push 14 sts at cent into HP next r.
K 1 r. Push 1 st at cent into HP
next and foll alt rs. 14 times in all
until 22 (26 30 33 37) sts rem.
RC 242.

Shape shoulder
C.off 5 (6 7 8 9) sts beg next and
foll alt rs. 3 times in all.
K 1 r. C.off rem 7 (8 9 9 10) sts.

Reset RC 116, working left side to
match.
AT SAME TIME on RC 148 and 184
mark. on 13th and 40th ns left of
cent. pocket.

SLEEVES
Col B, c.on in 1 x 1 rib, 61 (63 67
71 75) sts.
RC 000, T1/1, K 6 rs.
Col A, K 30 rs.
Trans sts to M/bed. Inc 1 st.
RC 000, MT, K 4 rs.
Inc 1 st both ends next and foll 4th
rs until 120 sts.
Cont to K until RC 138.

Shape top
C.off 6 sts beg next 2 rs.
C.off 3 sts beg next 2 rs.
Dec 1 st both ends next and foll
alt r. K 1 r.
Dec 1 st both ends next and foll
4th rs. 14 times in all.
K 1 r.
RC 200.
C.off 4 sts beg next 12 rs.
C.off rem 22 sts.
RC 212.

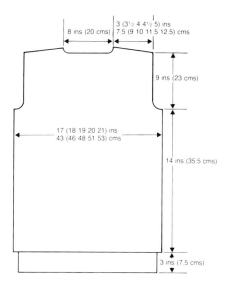

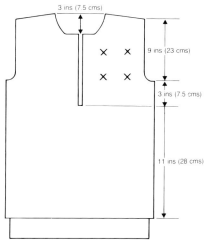

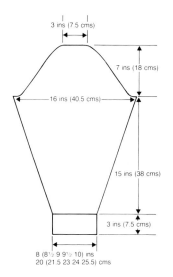

81

POCKET

Col B, c.on in 1 x 1 rib 27 sts.
RC 000, T2/2, K 6 rs. Col A, K 2 rs.
Trans sts to M/bed.
Col A, MT, K 26 rs.
C.off loosely.

FRONT BUTTON BAND

Col B, c.on in 1 x 1 rib, 71 sts.
RC 000, T2/2, K 6 rs. Col A, K 2 rs.
Trans sts to M/bed.
With wrong side facing, pick up sts
evenly along front opening.
MT, K 1 r. T10, K 1 r.

C. off with latch tool.

BUTTONHOLE BAND

K as for buttonband working 5
buttonholes along 3rd row.

COLLAR

Col B, c.on in 1 x 1 rib, 141 sts.
RC 000, T2/3, K 6 rs. Col A, T2/2, K
6 rs.
T1/2, K 6 rs. T1/1, K 12 rs.
RC 30.
Trans sts to M/bed.
With wrong side facing, pick up sts

from cent band around neck.
Placing 36 sts into HP, MT, K 1 r.
T10, K 1 r.
C.off with latch tool.
Rep for other side

TO MAKE UP

Join shoulder seams, sew on
pocket.
Insert sleeves, sew side and sleeve
seams.
Join band at cent.
Sew on buttons to front.
Press with very cool iron.

15

Blue-Heather
CARDIGAN SUIT

Sizes 34 (36 38 40 42) ins
(86 (91 97 102 107) cms) bust
36 (38 40 42 44) ins
(91 (97 102 107 112) cms) hip
Skirt length 29 ins (74 cms)

Materials 1 Cone Bramwell Lovat
4 ply: Col A
1 Cone Bramwell Pure Wool 4 ply:
Col B
7 buttons
Elastic to fit waist

Tension 30 sts × 42 rs = 4 ins
(10 cms) using col B over ss
Tension dials approx 7

36 sts × 40 rs = 4 ins (10 cms)
using Col A over rib patt
Tension dials approx 4/5

Needle arrangement:				
111	11111	11111	111	M/bed
11	11	11		Rib/bed

BACK
Col B, c.on in 1 × 1 rib, 131 (139
147 153 161) sts.
RC 000, T1/1, K 6 rs. Col A, K 30 rs.
RC 36.
Trans sts to M/bed. Inc 1 st.**
RC 000, MT, K 148 rs.

Shape armholes
C.off 6 sts beg next 2 rs.
C.off 3 sts beg next 2 rs.
Dec 1 st both ends next and foll
alt r.
K 1 r. 110 (118 126 132 140) sts.
RC 156.
Cont to K until RC 232.

Shape neck
Push 74 (80 84 87 91) sts at left
into HP or K back onto nylon cord.
Work on right side only.

Dec 1 st at cent next 10 rs.

Shape shoulder
C.off 5 (6 7 8 9) sts beg next and
foll alt rs. 3 times in all.
K 1 r. C.off rem 7 (8 9 9 10) sts.
Leave cent 46 sts in HP.
Return 32 (36 40 43 47) sts at left
to WP.
Work left side to match.

BACK NECK BAND
Trans sts to 1 × 1 rib.
RC 000, T1/1, Col A, K 10 rs.
Col B, K 6 rs.
C.off in rib.

LEFT FRONT
Col B, c.on in 1 × 1 rib, 59 (63 67
71 75) sts.
RC 000, T1/1, K as for back to **.
RC 000, MT, mark 13th and 40th rs

from left.
K 116 rs.

Shape front
Dec 1 st at left next and foll 3rd rs
until RC 148.

Shape armhole
Cont to dec at front edge
AT SAME TIME
C.off 6 sts beg next r. K 1 r.
C.off 3 sts beg next r. K 1 r.
Dec 1 st beg next and foll alt r.
Cont to dec at front edge until 22
(26 30 33 37) sts rem.
Cont to K until RC 242.

Shape shoulder
C.off 5 (6 7 8 9) sts beg next and
foll alt rs. 3 times in all.
K 1 r. C.off rem 7 (8 9 9 10) sts.

RIGHT FRONT

K as for left front rev shapings.

SLEEVES

Col B, c.on in 1 x 1 rib, 61 (63 67 71 75) sts
RC 000, T1/1, K as for back to **.
RC 000, MT, K 4 rs.
Inc 1 st both ends next and foll 4th rs until 120 sts.
Cont to K unril RC 138.

Shape top

C.off 6 sts beg next 2 rs.
C.off 3 sts beg next 2 rs.
Dec 1 st both ends next and foll alt r. K 1 r.
Dec 1 st both ends next and foll 4th rs. 14 times in all.
K 1 r.
RC 200.
C.off 4 sts beg next 12 rs.
C.off rem 22 sts.
RC 212.

POCKETS

Col B, c.on in 1 x 1 rib, 27 sts.
RC 000, T2/2, K 6 rs. Col A, K 2 rs.
Trans sts to M/bed.

Col A, MT, K 26 rs.
C.off loosely.

FRONT BUTTON BAND

Col B, c.on in 1 x 1 rib, 189 sts.
RC 000, T2/2, K 6 rs. Col A, K 10 rs.
Trans sts to M/bed.
With wrong side facing pick up sts evenly along left front.
MT, K 1 r. T10, K 1 r.
C.off with latch tool.

BUTTON HOLE BAND

K as above, working 7 buttonholes evenly along 9th r over 105 ns at left.

TO MAKE UP

Join shoulder seams.
Sew pockets between markers.
Sew side and sleeve seams.
Join neckband.
Press with very cool iron.
Sew on buttons.

Skirt

(Knit four panels)
Col B, c.on in 1 x 1 rib, 120 (127

134 141 148) sts.
Work circular c.on.
Trans sts to 5 x 2 rib (as diagram) leaving 3 sts in WP at both ends on M/bed to give ½ st at each end for seam.
RC 000, T4/5, K 270 rs.
Trans sts to M,/bed. K 1 r.
Rel work on WY.
Join panels leaving one open seam.

WAISTBAND

(Knit two)
Bring forward 104 (112 120 128 136) ns.
With wrong side facing, gather 2 panels onto ns.
RC 000, MT − 1, K 16 rs.
T10, K 1 r. MT − 1, K 16 rs.
T10, K 1 r. C.off loosely.

TO MAKE UP

Join last seam, fold waistband to inside and slip st into pos.
Thread elastic through waist.
Press with steam iron.

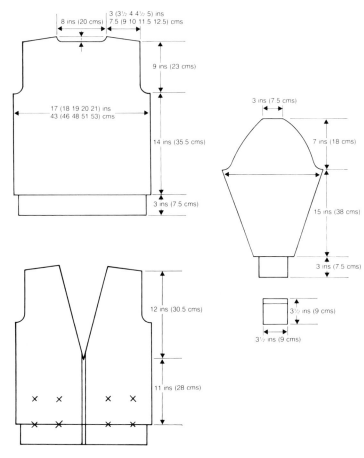

16

Lilac
COWL NECK SUIT

Sizes 34 (36 38 40 42) ins
(86 (91 97 102 107) cms) bust
36 (38 40 42 44) ins
(91 (97 102 107 112) cms) hip
Skirt length 28 ins (71 cms)

Materials 800 gms Bramwell Lovat
4 ply: Col A
100 gms Bramwell Lovat 4 ply:
Col B
Elastic to fit waist

Tension 30 sts × 42 rs = 4 ins
(10 cms) using Col A over ss
Tension dial approx 7

60 sts × 40 rs = 4 ins (10 cms)
using Col A over rib pattern
Tension dials approx 4/5

Needle arrangement:				
111	11111	11111	111	M/bed
11	11	11		Rib/bed

Skirt

(Knit four panels)
Col A, c.on in 1 × 1 rib, 120 (127
134 141 148) sts.
Work circular c.on.
Trans sts to 5 × 2 rib (as diagram),
leaving 3 sts in WP at both ends
on M/bed to give $\frac{1}{2}$ st each end for
seam.
RC 000, T4/5, K 270 rs.
Trans sts to M/bed.
K 1 r.
Rel work on WY.
Join panels leaving one open seam.

WAISTBAND

(Knit two)
Bring forward 104 (112 120 128
136) ns.

With wrong side facing, gather 2
panels onto ns.
RC 000, MT − 1, K 16 rs.
T10, K 1 r. MT − 1, K 16 rs.
T10, K 1 r.
C.off loosely.

TO MAKE UP

Join last seam, fold waistband to
inside and slip st into pos.
Thread elastic through waist.
Press with cool iron.

BACK

Col B, c.on in 1 × 1 rib, 127 (135
143 149 157) sts.
RC 000, T1/1, K 6 rs. Col A, K 30 rs.
RC 36.
Trans sts to M/bed. Inc 1 st.
RC 000, MT, K 148 rs.

Shape armholes

C.off 6 sts beg next 2 rs.

C.off 3 sts beg next 2 rs.
Dec 1 st both ends next and foll r.
K 1 r.
106 (114 122 128 136) sts.
RC 156. **
Cont to K until RC 232. *

Shape neck

Push 74 (78 82 85 89) sts at left
into HP or K back onto nylon cord.
Work on right side only.
Dec 1 st at cent next 10 rs.

Shape shoulder

C.off 5 (6 7 8 9) sts beg next and
foll alt rs. 3 times in all.
K 1 r.
C.off rem 7 (8 9 9 10) sts. Leave
cent 42 sts in HP.
Return 32 (36 40 43 47) sts at left
to WP.
Work left side to match.

Rel cent sts on WY.

FRONT

K as for back to **.
Cont to K until RC 190.

Shape neck

Push 64 (68 72 75 79) sts at left
into HP, or K back onto nylon
cord.
Work on right side only.
Dec 1 st at cent next and foll alt
rs. 20 times in all until 22 (26 30 33
37) sts rem.
Cont to K until RC 242.

Shape shoulder

C.off 5 (6 7 8 9) sts beg next and
foll alt rs. 3 times in all.
K 1 r.
C.off rem 7 (8 9 9 10) sts.
Leave cent 22 sts in HP.
Work left side to match.
Rel cent sts on WY.

SLEEVES

Col B, c.on in 1 x 1 rib, 61 (63 67
71 75) sts.
RC 000, T1/1, K 6 rs. Col A, K 30 rs.
Trans sts to M/bed. Inc 1 st.
RC 000, MT, K 4 rs.
Inc 1 st both ends next and foll 4th
rs until 120 sts.
Cont to K until RC 138.

Shape top

C.off 6 sts beg next 2 rs.
C.off 3 sts beg next 2 rs.
Dec 1 st both ends next and foll
alt r.
K 1 r.
Dec 1 st both ends next and foll
4th rs. 14 times in all.
K 1 r.
RC 200.
C.off 4 sts beg next 12 rs.
C.off rem 22 sts
RC 212.

NECKBAND

Col B, c.on in 1 x 1 rib, 163 sts.
RC 000, working in English
rib, T4/4, K 6 rs.
Col A, T4/4, K 30 rs.
T3/3, K 24 rs. T2/2, K 24 rs.
T3/3, K 24 rs. T4/4, K 35 rs.
RC 143.
Set carr for normal rib.
K 1 r.
Trans sts to M/bed.
With wrong side facing, pick up sts
evenly around neck.
MT, K 1 r. T10, K 1 r.
C.off with latch tool.

TO MAKE UP

Join shoulder seams.
Insert sleeves.
Sew side and sleeve seams.
Fold neckband to outside.
Press with cool iron.

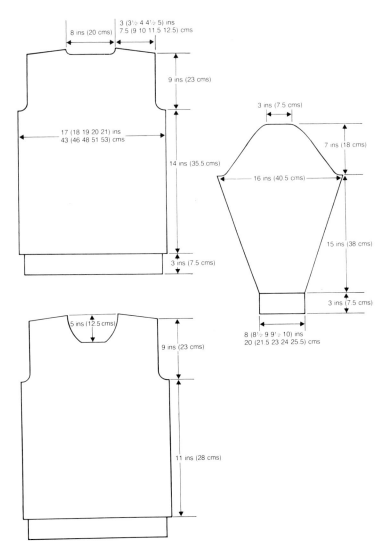

17
Navy-Blue
ZIP JACKET SUIT

Sizes 32 (34 36 38 40) ins
(81 (86 91 97 102) cms) bust
34 (36 38 40 42) ins
(86 (91 97 102 107) cms) hip
Skirt length 28 ins (71 cms)

Materials 500 gm Cone Bramwell
Lovat 4 ply: Col A
300 gms Bramwell Lovat 4 ply:
Col B
22 ins (56 cms) open end zip
Elastic to fit waist

Tension 30 sts × 42 rs = 4 ins
(10 cms) using Col A over ss
Tension dial approx 7

36 sts × 40 rs = 4 ins (10 cms)
using Col A over rib patt
Tension dials approx 4/5

Note Purl side is right side of
garment

Needle arrangement:				
111	11111	11111	111	M/bed
11	11	11		Rib/bed

Skirt
(Knit four panels)
Col A, c.on in 1 × 1 rib, 120 (127
134 141 148) sts.
Work circular c.on.
Trans sts to 5 × 2 rib (as diagram),
leaving 3 sts in WP at both ends
on M/bed to give ½ st each end for
seam.
RC 000, T4/5, K 270 rs.
Trans sts to M/bed.
K. 1 r.
Rel work on WY.
Join panels leaving one open seam.

WAISTBAND
(Knit two)
Bring forward 104 (112 120 128
136) ns.
With wrong side facing, gather 2
panels onto ns.
RC 000 MT-1 K 16 rs.
T10, K 1 r. MT-1, K 16 rs.
T10, K 1 r.
C.off loosely.

TO MAKE UP
Join last seam, fold waistband to
inside and slip st into pos.
Thread elastic through waist.
Press with cool iron.

BACK
Col A, c.on in 1 × 1 rib, 127 (135
143 149 157) sts.
RC 000, T1/1, K 40 rs.
Trans sts to M/bed.
Inc 1 st.
RC 000, MT, Col B, K 120 rs.

Shape armhole
C.off 6 sts beg next 2 rs.
C.off 3 sts beg next 2 rs.
Dec 1 st both ends next and foll
alt r.
K 1 r.
106 (114 122 128 136) sts.
Cont to K until RC 200.

Shape neck
Push 74 (78 82 85 89) sts at left
into HP, or K back onto nylon
cord.
Work on right side only.
Dec 1 st at neck next 10 rs.

Shape shoulder
C.off 5 (6 7 8 9) sts beg next and
foll alt rs. 3 times in all.
K 1 r.
C.off rem 7 (8 9 9 10) sts.

Leave cent 42 sts in HP.
Return 32 (36 40 43 47) sts at left into WP.
Work left side to match.
Rel cent sts on WY.

FRONT POCKET POUCH

C.on in WY, 66 (70 74 78 82) sts.
K few rs, carr at left.
K 1 r with nylon cord.
RC 000.
* Col A, MT, K 4 rs. Col B, K 2 rs. *
Rep * to * 3 times in all.
Col A, K 4 rs.
RC 22.
Cont to work in stripes.
C.off 4 sts beg next r.
K 1 r.
C.off 3 sts beg next and foll alt rs.
4 times in all.
K 1 r.
C.off 2 sts beg next and foll alt rs.
10 times in all.
28 (32 36 40 44) sts rem.
Cont to K until RC 66.
Rel work on WY.
K second pouch, rev shaping.

LEFT FRONT

Col A, c.on in 1 x 1 rib, 67 (71 73 77 81) sts.
RC 000, T1/1, K 40 rs.
Trans sts to M/bed.
Col B, dec 1 st at left. With knit side facing, pick up sts from bottom of pouch.
RC 000, MT, K 66 rs.
Working from the left, pick up 28 (32 36 40 44) sts from top of pouch.
Cont to K until RC 120.

Shape armhole

C.off 6 sts beg next r. K 1 r.
C.off 3 sts beg next r. K 1 r.
Dec 1 st both ends next and foll alt r. K 1 r.
55 (59 63 67 71) sts.
Cont to K until RC 190.

Shape neck

Push 13 (13 13 14 14) sts at left into HP next r. K 1 r.
At left, push 1 st into HP next 20 rs until 22 (26 30 33 37) sts rem.
Cont to K until RC 216.

Shape shoulder

C.off 5 (6 7 8 9) sts beg next and foll alt rs. 3 times in all.
K 1 r.
C.off rem 7 (8 9 9 10) sts.

RIGHT FRONT

K as for left, rev shaping.

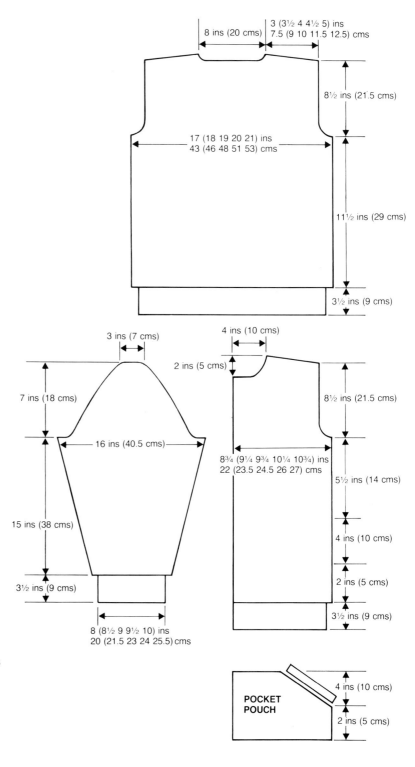

SLEEVES

Col A, c.on in 1 x 1 rib, 61 (63 67 71 75) sts.
RC 000, T1/1, K 40 rs.
Trans sts to M/bed.
Inc 1 st.
RC 000, MT, Col B, K 4 rs.
Inc 1 st both ends next and foll 4th rs until 120 sts
Cont to K until RC 138.

Shape top

Working in stripes: Col A, 4 rs. Col B, 2 rs.
C.off 6 sts beg next 2 rs.
C.off 3 sts beg next 2 rs.
Dec 1 st both ends next and foll alt r. K 1 r.

Carr at right.
Dec 1 st both ends next and foll 4th rs. 14 times in all.
K 1 r.
RC 200, c.off 4 sts beg next 12 rs.
C.off rem 22 sts.
RC 212.

NECKBAND

Col A, c.on in 1 x 1 rib, 141 sts.
RC 000, T2/3, K 4 rs. T2/2, K 4 rs.
T1/1, K 8 rs. T2/2, K 4 rs.
T2/3, K 4 rs.
Trans sts to M/bed.
With knit side facing, pick up sts evenly around neck.
MT, K 1 r. T10, K 1 r.
C.off with latch tool.

POCKET EDGES

Col A, c.on in 1 x 1 rib, 49 sts.
RC 000, T2/2, K 12 rs.
Trans sts to M/bed.
With knit side of pocket facing, pick up sts along shaped edge.
MT, K 1 r. T10, K 1 r.
C. off with latch tool.

TO MAKE UP

Join shoulder seams.
Insert sleeves, gathering at top.
Sew sleeve and side seams, sewing pouch edge into seam.
Fold neckband to inside and slip st into pos.
Sew pocket edge to garment.
Sew in zip.
Press with cool iron.

18

Grey-Orange
FAIRISLE
SWEATER SUIT

Sizes 32 (34 36 38 40 42) ins
(81 (86 91 97 102 107) cms) bust
34 (36 38 40 42 44) ins
(86 (91 97 102 107 112) cms) hip
Skirt length 28 ins (71 cms)

Materials 1 Cone Bramwell Duo
Spun (2 ply): Col A
1 Cone 4-ply Acrylic: Col B
Card as shown
Elastic to fit waist

Tension 31 sts × 49 rs = 4 ins
(10 cms) using Col A over full n rib
Tension dials approx 4/4

30 sts × 40 rs = 4 ins (10 cms)
using both yarns over fairisle patt
Tension dial approx 7

Skirt
(Knit two panels)
Col A, c.on in full n rib, 148 (156
164 172 180 188) sts.
Work c.on rows.
RC 000, MT, K 204 rs.
Mark both edges.
Dec 1 st both ends next and foll
5th rs until 100 (108 116 124 132
140) sts.
Cont to K until RC 330.
Mark both edges.
K 14 rs. T8/8, K 1 r.
MT, K 14 rs.
C.off loosely.

TO MAKE UP
Join side seams.
Fold waistband to inside and slip st
into pos.
Thread elastic through waist.

Sweater

BACK
Insert card and lock to K row 1.
Col B, c.on in 1 × 1 rib, 131 (137
145 151 159 165).

RC 000, T2/2, K 30 rs.
Trans sts to M/bed.
RC 000, MT, working in fairisle, Col
B, feeder 1, Col A, feeder 2, K 116
(120 122 124 126 126) rs. *

Shape raglan
RC 000, c.off 6 (6 6 6 6 7) sts beg
next 2 rs.
Dec 1 st both ends next and foll
4th rs. 3 times in all.
K 1 r.
Dec 1 st both ends next and foll
alt rs until 37 (37 37 39 43 47) sts
rem.
RC 88 (94 102 106 110 110).
Mark cent st.
Rel cent sts on WY.

FRONT
K as for back to *.

Shape raglan
RC 000, c.off 6 (6 6 6 6 7) sts beg
next 2 rs.
Dec 1 st both ends next and foll
alt rs until 71 (71 71 81 83 87) sts
rem.

Shape neck
MARK CARD ROW No and
cent st.
C.off cent 19 (19 19 21 21 21) sts.
Place all sts left cent into HP, or K
back onto nylon cord.
Work on right side only, keeping
raglan shaping correct dec 1 st at
neck next 12 (12 12 12 14 16) rs.
Cont to dec at Raglan until all sts
have been decreased.
RC 78 (84 92 96 100 100).
Reset RC.
Work left side to match.

SLEEVES

Insert card and lock to K row 1.
Col B, c.on in 1 x 1 rib, 61 (63 65 67 69 71) sts.
RC 000, T2/2, K 30 rs.
Trans sts to M/bed. Inc 1 st.
RC 000, MT, working in fairisle, K 2 rs.
Inc 1 st both ends next and foll 4th rs until 108 (118 126 128 130 132) sts.
Cont to K until RC 140.

Shape raglan

RC 000, c.off 6 (6 6 6 6 7) sts beg next 2 rs.
Dec 1 st both ends next and foll alt rs until 20 (22 24 22 20 20) sts rem.

Shape top

C.off 10 (12 14 12 10 10) sts beg next r.
K 1 r, carr at right.
Dec 1 st both ends next and foll alt rs until all sts have been dec.
RC 88 (94 102 106 110 110).
Rep for second sleeve, rev top shaping.

COLLAR

Col A, c.on in full n bed rib, 136 sts.
Work circular c.on.
RC 000, T4/4, K 10 rs. T3/3, K 20 rs.
T4/4 K 8 rs.
RC 38.
Trans sts to M/bed.
* With the purl side facing, pick up sts from cent front to cent back. including tops of sleeves.*
Push ns at left into HP.
T5, K 3 rs. T10, K 1 r.
C.off with latch tool.
Rep from * to * for other side.

TO MAKE UP

Join raglans, sew side and sleeve seams. Sew 3 rs of s/s inside collar to garment with slip st.
Fold collar to outside.
Press lightly.

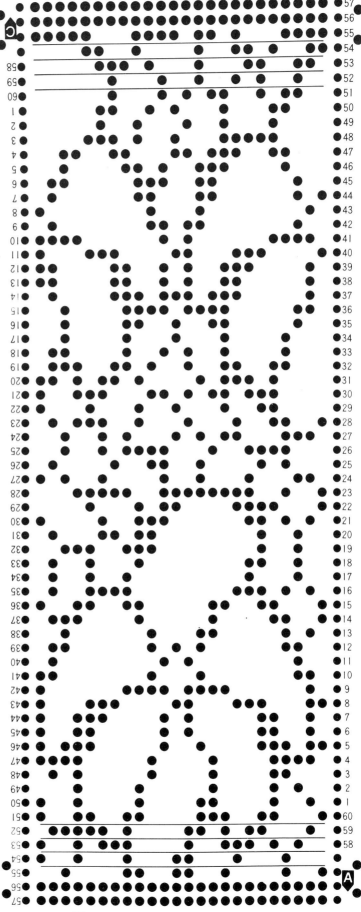

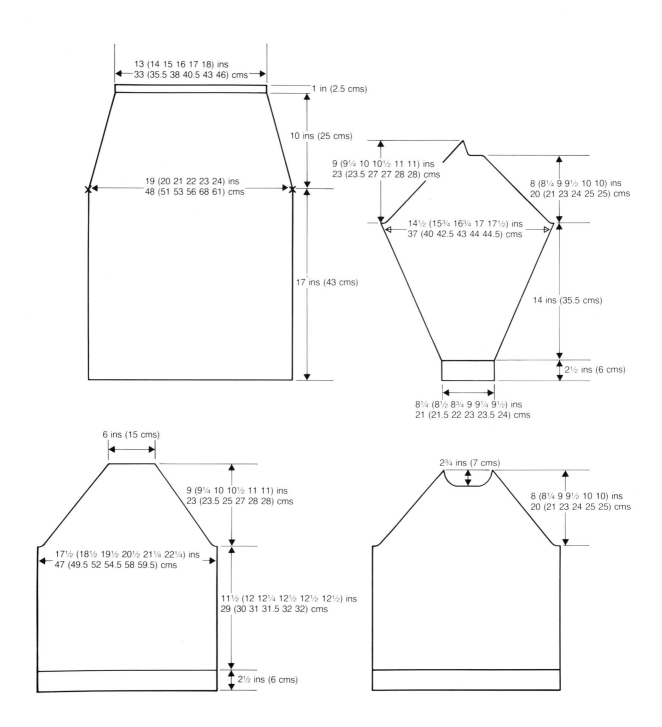

13 (14 15 16 17 18) ins
33 (35.5 38 40.5 43 46) cms

1 in (2.5 cms)

10 ins (25 cms)

19 (20 21 22 23 24) ins
48 (51 53 56 68 61) cms

17 ins (43 cms)

9 (9¼ 10 10½ 11 11) ins
23 (23.5 27 27 28 28) cms

8 (8¼ 9 9½ 10 10) ins
20 (21 23 24 25 25) cms

14½ (15¾ 16¾ 17 17½) ins
37 (40 42.5 43 44 44.5) cms

14 ins (35.5 cms)

2½ ins (6 cms)

8¼ (8½ 8¾ 9 9¼ 9½) ins
21 (21.5 22 23 23.5 24) cms

6 ins (15 cms)

9 (9¼ 10 10½ 11 11) ins
23 (23.5 25 27 28 28) cms

17½ (18½ 19½ 20½ 21¼ 22¼) ins
47 (49.5 52 54.5 58 59.5) cms

11½ (12 12¼ 12½ 12½ 12½) ins
29 (30 31 31.5 32 32) cms

2½ ins (6 cms)

2¾ ins (7 cms)

8 (8¼ 9 9½ 10 10) ins
20 (21 23 24 25 25) cms

Winter

19

Red
BLAZER
JACKET SUIT

Sizes 32 (34 36 38 40 42) ins
(81 (86 91 97 102 107) cms) bust
34 (36 38 40 42 44) ins
(86 (91 97 102 107 112) cms) hip
Skirt length 30 ins (76 cms)

Materials 1 Cone Bramwell
Astrakan: Col A
250 gms matching Silky (2/30s
Acrylic Brights): Col A
Elastic to fit waist
11 buttons

Tension 32 sts × 56 rs = 4 ins
(10 cms) using 1 end both Col A
Tension dial approx 3

Note Purl side is right side of
garment

Skirt
C.on in WY 195 sts.
K few rs carr at left.
K 1 r with nylon cord.
Using 1 end each yarn, RC 000,
MT, K 20 rs.
Always taking yarn round last ns in
HP, push 125 sts at left into HP.
Push 5 sts at left into HP next and
foll alt rs. 13 times in all.
Push 5 sts at right into WP next
and foll alt rs. 13 times in all.
* RC 000.
Push 125 ns at left into HP.
Push 5 sts at left into HP next and
foll alt rs. 13 times in all.
RC 26.
Push 5 sts at right back into WP
next and foll alt rs. 13 times in all.
RC 52.
K 42 (46 48 50 54 56) rs across all
ns.

RC 94 (98 100 102 106 108).
Bring 125 ns at left into HP.
Push 5 sts at left into HP next and
foll alt rs. 13 times in all.
Push 5 sts at right into WP next
and foll alt rs. 13 times in all.
RC 146 (150 152 154 158 160). **
K 42 (46 48 50 54 56) rs across all
ns. RC 188 (196 200 204 212 216).
Bring 125 ns at left into HP.
Push 5 sts left into HP next and foll
alt rs. 13 times in all.
Push 5 sts right into WP next and
foll alt rs. 13 times in all.
RC 240 (248 252 256 264 278). ***
Reset RC 000.

Work 5 panels from * to ***, then K
from * to **.
K 22 (26 28 30 34 36) rs.

Join back seam
Pick up first row of knitting placing
sts over last row.
MT, K 1 r. T10, K 1 r.
C.off with latch tool.

WAISTBAND
Bring forward 104 (112 120 128 138
144) ns.
With K side facing, pick up sts
evenly from front or back waist.
MT, K 16 rs. T10, K 1 r.
MT, K 16 rs. T10, K 1 r.

C.off with latch tool.

TO MAKE UP

Join waistband and slip st to inside.
Thread elastic through waist.
Steam press.

Jacket

BACK

C.on in WY 136 (144 152 160 168
176) sts.
K few rs carr at left.
K 1 r with nylon cord.
Using both yarns, RC 000, MT,
K 10 rs.
MT + 3, K 1 r. MT, K 10 rs.
Turn up hem.
RC 000, MT, K 148 rs.

Shape armholes

C.off 6 sts beg next 2 rs.
C.off 3 sts beg next 2 rs.
Dec 1 st both ends next and foll
alt rs. 2 times in all until 114 (122
130 138 146 154) sts rem.
Cont to K until RC 262.

Shape back neck

Push 86 (90 94 98 102 106) sts at
left into HP or K back onto nylon
cord.
Work on right side only.
Dec 1 st at neck next 6 rs.
K 4 rs.
RC 272.

Shape shoulders

C.off 4 (4 6 7 8 9) sts beg next and
foll alt rs. 3 times in all.
C.off 4 (6 6 7 8 9) sts beg next r.
K 1 r.
C.off rem 6 (8 6 6 6 6) sts.
Leave cent 58 sts in HP.
Work left side to match.
Rel cent sts on WY.

RIGHT FRONT

On rows 56 and 168, counting
from right mark 21st and 48th ns.

C.on in WY 64 (68 72 76 80 84) sts.
K few rs, carr at left
K 1 r with nylon cord.
RC 000, MT, K 10 rs. MT − 3, K 1 r.
MT, K 10 rs.
Turn up hem.
RC 000, MT, K 148 rs.

Shape armholes

C.off 6 sts beg next r. K 1 r.
C.off 3 sts beg next r. K 1 r.
Dec 1 st beg next and foll alt r
until 53 (57 61 65 69 73) sts rem.
Cont to K until RC 232.

Shape neck

Push 13 sts at left into HP next r.
K 1 r.
Push 1 st at left into HP next and
foll alt rs. 18 times in all.
Cont to K until RC 272.

Shape shoulders

C.off 4 (4 6 7 8 9) sts beg next and
foll alt rs. 3 times in all.
C.off 4 (6 6 7 8 9) sts beg next r.
K 1 r. C.off rem 6 (8 6 6 6 6) sts.
Rel sts held in HP onto WY.

Rep for left front, reversing
shaping.

SLEEVES

C.on in WY 72 (72 72 80 80 88) sts.
K few rs, carr at left.
K 1 r with nylon cord.
RC 000, MT, K 10 rs. MT + 3, K 1 r.
MT, K 10 rs.
Turn up hem.
RC 000, MT, K 4 rs.
Inc 1 st both ends next and foll 5th
(5th 5th 6th 6th 7th) rs until
144 sts.
Cont to K until RC 214.

Shape top

C.off 6 sts beg next 2 rs.
C.off 3 sts beg next 2 rs.
Dec 1 st both ends next and foll

alt rs. 2 times in all.
RC 222.
Dec 1 st both ends next and foll
4th rs. 20 times in all.
K 1 r. RC 300, 82 sts.
C.off 4 sts beg next 12 rs.
C.off 5 sts beg next 2 rs.
C.off rem 24 sts.
RC 314.

FRONT BAND

C.on in WY 140 sts.
RC 000, MT − 1, K 10 rs.
MT + 4, K 1 r. MT − 1, K 10 rs.
Turn up hem.
With knit side of garment facing,
pick up stitches down front.
MT, K 1 r. T10, K 1 r.
C.off with latch tool.

BUTTONHOLE BAND

K as above working 7 buttonholes
evenly along 5th and 17th rs.

NECKBAND

C.on in WY 144 sts.
RC 000, MT − 1, K 20 rs.
MT + 4, K 1 r. MT − 1, K 20 rs.
Turn up hem.
With knit side facing, pick up 6 sts
from front band, 31 sts from front
neck, 70 sts across back, 31 sts
down front, 6 sts from band.
MT, K 1 r. T10, K 1 r.
C.off with latch tool.

MOCK POCKET FLAPS

(Knit 4)
C.on by hand 28 sts.
RC 000, K 14 rs.
C.off loosely.

TO MAKE UP

Sew pocket flaps between markers.
Join shoulder seams.
Insert sleeves gathering at top.
Sew side and sleeve seams.
Press with steam iron.
Sew on buttons.

1 SKIRT PANEL

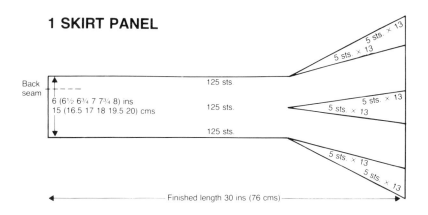

Back seam

6 (6½ 6¾ 7 7¾ 8) ins
15 (16.5 17 18 19.5 20) cms

125 sts

125 sts.

125 sts.

5 sts. × 13

5 sts. × 13

5 sts. × 13

5 sts. × 13

5 sts. × 13

5 sts. × 13

Finished length 30 ins (76 cms)

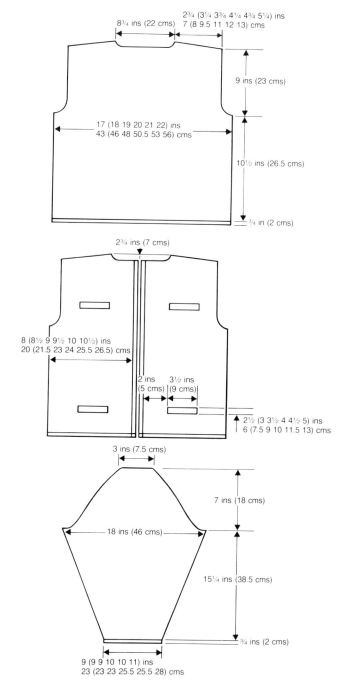

2¾ (3¼ 3¾ 4¼ 4¾ 5¼) ins
7 (8 9.5 11 12 13) cms

8¾ ins (22 cms)

9 ins (23 cms)

17 (18 19 20 21 22) ins
43 (46 48 50.5 53 56) cms

10½ ins (26.5 cms)

¾ in (2 cms)

2¾ ins (7 cms)

8 (8½ 9 9½ 10 10½) ins
20 (21.5 23 24 25.5 26.5) cms

2 ins
(5 cms)

3½ ins
(9 cms)

2½ (3 3½ 4 4½ 5) ins
6 (7.5 9 10 11.5 13) cms

3 ins (7.5 cms)

7 ins (18 cms)

18 ins (46 cms)

15¼ ins (38.5 cms)

¾ ins (2 cms)

9 (9 9 10 10 11) ins
23 (23 23 25.5 25.5 28) cms

20

Red-Black
WAISTED
JACKET SUIT

Sizes 32 (34 36 38 40 42) ins
(81 (86 91 97 102 107) cms) bust
34 (36 38 40 42 44) ins
(86 (91 97 102 107 112) cms) hip
Skirt length 30 ins (76 cms)

Materials 1 Cone Bramwell
Astrakan: Col A
250 gms Silky (2/30s Acrylic
Brights): Col A
1 Cone DB Matchmaker: Col B
Elastic to fit waist
20 ins (50 cms) zip for front

Tension 32 sts × 56 rs = 4 ins
(10 cms) using 1 end both Col A
Tension dial approx 3

Note Purl side is right side of
garment.

Skirt

C.on in WY 195 sts.
K few rs, carr at left.
K 1 r with nylon cord.
RC 000.
MT using both ends Col A.
* Push 125 ns left into HP.
Always taking yarn round last ns in
HP at left, push 5 sts into HP next
and foll alt rs. 13 times in all.
RC 26.
Push 5 sts at right back into WP
next and foll alt rs. 13 times in all.
RC 52.
K 42 (46 48 50 54 56) rs across all
ns.
RC 94 (98 100 102 106 108).
Bring 125 ns at left into HP.
Push 5 sts at left into HP next and
foll alt rs. 13 times in all.
Push 5 sts at right into WP next
and foll alt rs. 13 times in all.
RC 146 (150 152 154 158 160).
K 42 (46 48 50 54 56) rs across
all ns.
RC 188 (196 200 204 212 216).

Bring 125 ns at left into HP.
Push 5 sts left into HP next and foll
alt rs. 13 times in all.
Push 5 sts right into WP next and
foll alt rs. 13 times in all.
RC 240 (248 252 256 264 278). *

Reset RC 000, work 5 more panels
from * to *.

JOIN BACK SEAM
Pick up first row of knitting placing
sts over last row.
MT, K 1 r. T10, K 1 r.
C.off with latch tool.

WAISTBAND

Bring forward 104 (112 120 128 138
144) ns.
With K side facing, pick up sts
evenly from front or back waist.
MT, K 16 rs. T10, K 1 r.
MT, K 16 rs. T10, K 1 r.

C.off with latch tool.

TO MAKE UP

Join waistband and slip st to inside,
thread elastic through waist.
Steam press.

Jacket

BACK

Using 2 ends Col B, c.on in 1 × 1
rib, 135 (143 151 159 167 175) sts.
RC 000, T1/1, K 48 rs.
Trans sts to M/bed.
Inc 1 st.
Using both ends Col A, RC 000,
MT, K 100 rs.

Shape armholes

C.off 6 sts beg next 2 rs.
C. off 3 sts beg next 2 rs.
Dec 1 st both ends next and foll
alt r until 114 (122 130 138 146

154) sts rem.
Cont to K until RC 216.

Shape neck

Push 86 (90 94 98 102 106) sts at
left into HP or knit back onto
nylon cord.
Work on right side only.
Dec 1 st at neck next 6 rs.
K until RC 226.

Shape shoulders

C.off 4 (4 6 7 8 9) sts beg next and
foll alt rs. 3 times in all.
K 1 r.
C.off 4 (6 6 7 8 9) sts beg next r.
K 1 r. C.off rem 6 (8 6 6 6 6) sts.
Leave cent 58 sts in HP.
Work left side to match.
Rel cent sts on WY.

LEFT FRONT

On row 126 counting from left,
mark 21st and 48th ns.
Using 2 ends Col B, c.on in 1 × 1
rib, 69 (71 75 79 83 87) sts.
RC 000, T1/T1, K 48 rs.
Trans sts to M/bed. Inc 1 st.
RC 000, MT, Col A, K 100 rs.

Shape armhole

C.off 6 sts beg next r. K 1 r.
C.off 3 sts beg next r. K 1 r.
Dec 1 st beg next and foll alt r
until 57 (61 65 69 73 77) sts.
Cont to K until RC 196.

Shape front neck

Push 21 sts at left into HP next r.
K 1 r.
Push 1 st at left into HP next and
foll alt rs. 14 times in all.
22 (26 30 34 38 42) sts rem.
RC 226.

Shape shoulder

C.off 4 (4 6 7 8 9) sts beg next and
foll alt rs. 3 times in all.
C.off 4 (6 6 7 8 9) sts beg next r.
K 1 r. C.off rem 6 (8 6 6 6 6) sts.

Work left front, reversing shaping.

SLEEVES

Using 2 ends Col B, c.on in 1 × 1
rib, 65 (67 69 71 73 75) sts.
RC 000, T1/1, K 48 rs.
Trans sts to M/bed. Inc 1 st.
RC 000, Col A, K 4 rs.
Inc 1 st both ends next and foll 4th
rs until 144 sts.
Cont to K until RC 170.

Shape top

C.off 6 sts beg next 2 rs.
C.off 3 sts beg next 2 rs.

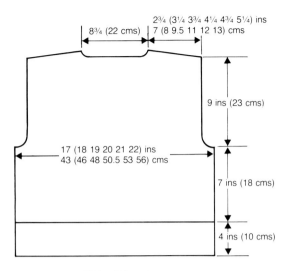

2¾ (3¼ 3¾ 4¼ 4¾ 5¼) ins
7 (8 9.5 11 12 13) cms

8¾ (22 cms)

9 ins (23 cms)

17 (18 19 20 21 22) ins
43 (46 48 50.5 53 56) cms

7 ins (18 cms)

4 ins (10 cms)

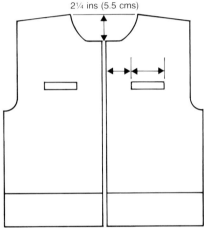

2¼ ins (5.5 cms)

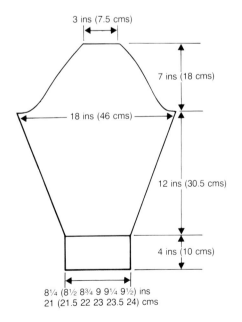

3 ins (7.5 cms)

7 ins (18 cms)

18 ins (46 cms)

12 ins (30.5 cms)

4 ins (10 cms)

8¼ (8½ 8¾ 9 9¼ 9½) ins
21 (21.5 22 23 23.5 24) cms

Skirt as Pattern 19

Dec 1 st both ends next and foll alt r. K 1 r.
RC 178.
Dec 1 st both ends next and foll 4th rs. 20 times in all. K 1 r.
RC 256, 82 sts rem.
C.off 4 sts beg next 12 rs.
C.off 5 sts beg next 2 rs.
C.off rem 24 sts.
RC 270.

MOCK POCKET FLAPS
Using 2 ends Col B, c.on by hand

28 sts.
RC 000, T5, K 14 rs.
C.off loosely.

COLLAR
Using 2 ends Col B, c.on in 1 x 1 rib, 155 sts.
RC 000, T3/3, K 10 rs.
T2/2, K 10 rs. T1/1, K 10 rs.
T2/2, K 10 rs. T3/3, K 9 rs.
T4/3, K 1 r.
With knit side facing, pick up sts

evenly around neck.
MT, K 1 r. T10, K 1 r.
C.off with latch tool.

TO MAKE UP
Join shoulder seams.
Insert sleeves gathering at top.
Sew side and sleeve seams.
Sew on pocket flaps between markers.
Sew in zip.
Press with steam iron.

21

Shades of Blue
WOVEN JACKET SUIT

Sizes 32 (34 36 38 40) ins
(81 (86 91 97 102 cms) bust
34 (36 38 40 42) ins
(86 (91 97 102 107) cms) hip

Materials 3 Cones Atkinsons 2-ply
Wool: Col A
200 grms each Atkinsons Impulse:
Cols B, C, D
22 ins (56 cms) Zip
Card as shown
Elastic to fit waist

Tension 24 sts × 60 rs = 4 ins
(10 cms) using 1 end Col A over
weaving pattern in feeder 1 and
Impulse as weaving yarn.
Tension dial approx 4

37 sts × 50 rs = 4 ins (10 cms) using
1 end Col A over rib pattern
Tension dials approx 2/3

Note Use 2 ends Col A for all
welts, 1 end for weaving pattern

Needle arrangement:	
1111111111111	M/bed
11 111 111 11	Rib/bed

WEAVING PATTERN
(Col B: Plum, Col C: Green, Col D:
Lilac)
* Col C, K 2 rs. Col B, K 2 rs. Col D,
K 4 rs.
Col B, K 20 rs. Col D, K 4 rs. Col B,
K 4 rs.
Col C, K 10 rs. Col B, K 10 rs. Col
D, K 4 rs.
Col B, K 2 rs. Col C, K 2 rs. **

Skirt
(Knit 2(2 2 2 3) panels)

Col A, c.on in full n rib, 167 (178
186 198 70) sts.

Work c.on rs.
Trans sts from rib bed to 3 × 1 rib.
RC 000, MT, K 226 rs.
Mark both edges.
K 18 rs.
MT + 2/2, K 1 r. MT − 1/1, K 18 rs.
C.off loosely.

TO MAKE UP
Join seams, fold waistband to
inside and slip st into pos.
Thread elastic through waist.
Press very lightly.

Body
Insert card and lock to K row 1.
INTERFACING
Col A, c.on by hand 108 sts.
MT-3, K 12 rs.
RC 000, MT, AT SAME TIME
Work weaving patt throughout
from * to ** and K 35 rs.

Inc 1 st at right next and foll 3rd rs.
12 times in all until 120 sts.
RC68.

FRONT SHOULDER
K 53 (61 67 75 83)
POCKET OPENING at left.
C.off 30 sts beg next r.
K until RC 136 (144 150 158 166).

ARMHOLE
C.off 60 sts at right beg next r.
C.on 30 sts at left beg next r.
C.on 60 sts at right beg next r.

BACK SHOULDER
K until RC 204 (220 232 248 264).

SHAPE NECK
Dec 1 st at right next 6 rs.
K 126 rs.
Inc 1 st at right next 6 rs.
RC 340 (356 368 384 400).

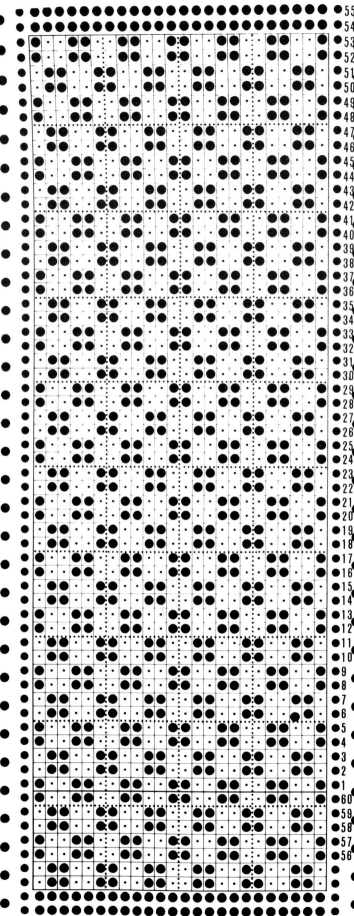

BACK SHOULDER

K 68 (76 82 90 98) rs.
RC 408 (432 450 474 498).

ARMHOLE AND POCKET OPENING

C.off 60 sts at right beg next r.
C.off 30 sts at left beg next r.
C.on 60 sts at right beg next r.
K 14 rs, carr at left.
C.on 30 sts at left beg next r.

FRONT SHOULDER

K until RC 476 (508 532 564 596).

Shape front

Dec 1 st at right next and foll 3rd
rs. 12 times in all until 108 sts.
K until RC 544 (576 600 632 664).
Col A only, MT + 3, K 12 rs.
C.off loosely.

SLEEVES

Insert card and lock to K row 1.
Using 2 ends Col A, c.on in 1 × 1
rib, 63 (67 71 75 79) sts.
RC 000, T2/2, K 48 rs.
Trans sts to M/bed.
Inc 1 st.
Working in weaving patt, RC 000,
MT, K 4 rs.
Inc 1 st both ends next and foll 6th
rs until 120 sts.
Cont to K until RC 170.
C.off very loosely.

POCKET EDGES

Using 2 ends Col A, c.on in 1 × 1
rib, 33 sts.
RC 000, T2/2, K 14 rs. T8/8, K 1 r.
T2/2, K 14 rs.
Trans sts to M/bed.
With wrong side facing, pick up sts
from front pocket opening.
MT + 3, K 1 r. T10, K 1 r.
C. off with latch tools.
Fold to inside.

POCKET LINING

Bring forward 33 ns.
With wrong side facing, pick up sts
from back pocket opening.
Col A, 1 end, MT + 3, K 71 rs. T10,
K 1 r.
C.off loosely.

BACK WELT

Using 2 ends Col A, c.on in 1 × 1
rib 139 (147 155 163 171) sts.
RC 000, T2/2, K 48 rs.
Trans sts to M/bed.
With wrong side facing, pick up sts
evenly along back, including
pocket top.
T7, K 1 r. T10, K 1 r.
C.off with latch tool.

FRONT WELT

Using 2 ends Col A, c.on in 1 × 1
rib, 63 (67 71 75 79) sts.
RC 000, T2/2, K 48 rs.
Trans sts to M/bed.
With wrong side facing, pick up sts
evenly from front.
T7, K 1 r. T10, K 1 r.
C.off with latch tool.

NECKBAND

Using 2 ends Col A c.on in 1 × 1
rib, 149 sts.
RC 000, T2/2, K 20 rs. T1/1, K 10 rs.
T5/6 K 1 r. T1/1, K 10 rs.
T2/2, K 20 rs. T5/6, K 1 r.
Trans sts to M/bed.
With wrong side facing, pick up 39
sts from front, 72 sts along back,
39 sts from front.
T7, K 1 r. T10, K 1 r.
C.off with latch tool.

TO MAKE UP

Join shoulder seams.
Sew pocket linings to front.
Fold pocket tops to inside and slip
st into pos.
Insert sleeves.
Sew sleeve seams.
Fold neckband to inside and slip st
into pos.
Press.
Sew zip to front.

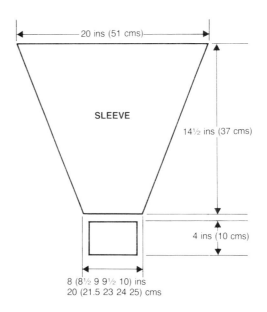

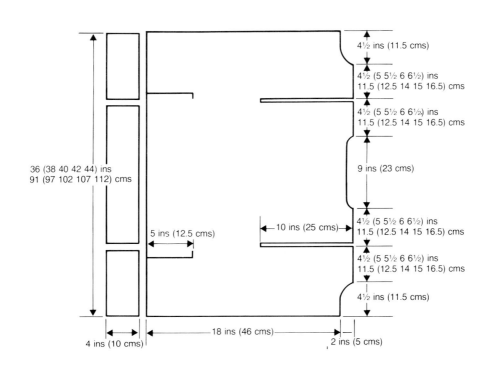

22
Shades of Rust
WOVEN SWEATER SUIT

Sizes 32 (34 36 38 40) ins
(81 (86 91 97 102) cms) bust
34 (36 38 40 42) ins
(86 (91 97 102 107) cms) hip
Skirt length 29 ins (74 cms)

Materials 1 Cone Atkinsons 2-ply
Pure Wool: Col A
100 gms each Atkinson Impulse:
Cols B and C
1 Cone Atkinson 2-ply Pure Wool:
Col D
Card as shown
Elastic to fit waist

Tension 24 sts × 60 rs = 4 ins
(10 cms) using 1 end Col A in
Feeder 1 and Impulse as weaving
yarn over weaving pattern
Tension dial approx 4

37 sts × 50 rs = 4 ins (10 cms)
Using 1 end Col D over rib pattern
Tension dials approx 2/3

Note Use 2 ends Col A for all
welts, 1 end for weaving pattern

Needle arrangement:				
111	11111	11111	111	M/bed
11	11	11		Rib/bed

Weaving pattern
* Col A in feeder 1, Col B, K 2 rs.
Col A in feeder 1, Col C, K 4 rs. *

Skirt
(Knit four panels)
Col D, c.on in 1 × 1 rib, 120 (127
134 141 148) sts.
Work circular c.on.
Trans sts to 5 × 2 rib (as diagram),
leaving 3 sts in WP on both ends

on M/bed to give ½ st at each end
for seam.
RC 000, T4/5, K 270 rs.
Trans sts to M/bed. K 1 r.
Rel work on WY.
Join panels leaving one open seam.

WAISTBAND

(Knit two)
Bring forward 104 (112 120 128
136) ns.
With wrong side facing gather 2
panels onto ns.
RC 000, MT-1, K 16 rs.
T10, K 1 r. MT-1, K 16 rs.
T10, K 1 r. C.off loosely.

TO MAKE UP

Join last seam, fold waistband to
inside and slip st into pos.
Thread elastic through waist.
Press.

Jacket

BACK

Insert card and lock to K row 1.
Col A, c.on by hand 88 sts (80 o 8).
RC 000, MT, working in weaving
patt, K 2 rs.

Shape armhole

Inc 1 st at right next and foll alt rs.
8 times in all.
C.on 64 sts (e method) at right.
RC 18.
K 46 (54 62 68 76) rs. *

Shape neck

Dec 1 st at right next 6 rs.
K 116 rs. Inc 1 st at right next 6 rs.
RC 192 (198 206 214 222) **.
K 46 (54 62 68 76) rs.
C.off 64 sts at right.
Dec 1 st at next and foll alt rs. 8
times in all.
K 2 rs.
RC 256 (268 284 300 316).
C.off loosely.

FRONT

K as for back to *.

Shape neck

C.off 5 sts beg next and foll alt rs.
4 times in all.
K 1 r.
RC 72 (78 86 94 102).
C.off 4 sts beg next and foll alt r.
K 1 r.
C.off 2 sts beg next and foll alt rs.
26 times in all.
80 sts.
RC 128 (136 144 150 158).

C. on 2 sts (e method) at right next and foll alt rs. 26 times in all.
C.on 4 sts (e method) at right next and foll alt r. K 1 r.
C.on 5 sts beg next and foll alt rs. 4 times in all.
RC 192 (198 206 214 222).
K as for back from **.

SLEEVES

Insert card and lock to K row 1.
Using 2 ends Col A, c.on in 1 x 1 rib, 61 (65 69 73 77) sts.
RC 000, T2/2, K 40 rs.
Trans sts to M/bed. Inc 1 st.
RC 000, working in weaving pattern, MT, K 2 rs.
Inc 1 st both ends next and foll 4th rs until 144 sts.
Cont to K until RC 202.

Shape top

Dec 1 st both ends next and foll alt rs. 8 times in all.
RC 218.
C.off loosely.

NECKBAND

Using 2 ends Col A, c.on in 1 x 1 rib, 153 sts.
*RC 000, T 2/2, K 15 rs.
T7/8, K 1 r. T2/2, K 15 rs.
T 4/5, K 1 r. Trans sts to M/bed. *
With wrong side facing, pick up 85 sts from cent V to shoulder, 68 sts across back.
MT, K 1 r. T10, K 1 r.
C.off loosely.

SECOND SIDE

C.on in 1 x 1 rib, 85 sts.
K as for first side from * to * picking up sts from cent V to shoulder.

WELTS

Using 2 ends Col A, c.on in 1 x 1 rib, 135 (143 151 159 167) sts.
RC 000, T2/2, K 40 rs.
Trans sts to M/bed.
With wrong side facing, pick up sts from front or back waist.

TO MAKE UP

Join shoulder seams, insert sleeves.
Sew side and sleeve seams.
Fold neckband to inside and slip st into pos.
Press.

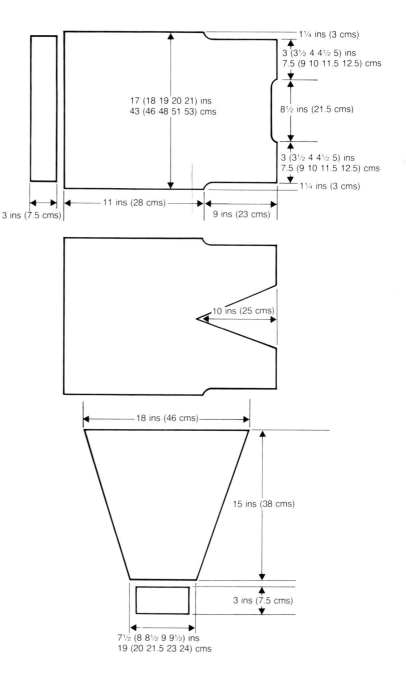

1¼ ins (3 cms)

3 (3½ 4 4½ 5) ins
7.5 (9 10 11.5 12.5) cms

17 (18 19 20 21) ins
43 (46 48 51 53) cms

8½ ins (21.5 cms)

3 (3½ 4 4½ 5) ins
7.5 (9 10 11.5 12.5) cms

1¼ ins (3 cms)

3 ins (7.5 cms)

11 ins (28 cms)

9 ins (23 cms)

10 ins (25 cms)

18 ins (46 cms)

15 ins (38 cms)

3 ins (7.5 cms)

7½ (8 8½ 9 9½) ins
19 (20 21.5 23 24) cms

23
Shades of Blue-Claret
WOVEN MOHAIR SUIT

Sizes 32 (34 36 38 40) ins
(81 86 91 97 102) cms) bust
36 (38 40 42 44) ins
(91 97 102 107 112) cms) hip
Skirt length 29 ins (74 cms)

Materials 3 Cones 2-ply Pure
Wool: Col A
1 Cone BK 4-ply Mohair: Col B
Card as shown
Elastic to fit waist

Tension 26 sts × 44 rs = 4 ins
(10 cms) using 1 end Col A in
feeder 1 and Mohair as weaving
yarns over weaving pattern
Tension dial approx 7

37 sts × 50 rs = 4 ins (10 cms)
using Col A over rib pattern
Tension dials approx 2/3

Note Woven side of sweater is
right side of garment
Use 2 ends of Col A for all welts, 1
end for weaving pattern

Needle arrangement:				
111	11111	11111	111	M/bed
11	11	11		Rib/bed

Skirt

(Knit four panels)
Col A c.on in 1 × 1 rib, 120 (127
134 141 148) sts.
Work circular c.on.
Trans sts to 5 × 2 rib (as diagram),
leaving 3 sts in WP at both ends
on M/bed to give ½ st at each end
for seam.
RC 000, T4/5, K 270 rs.
Trans sts to M/bed. K 1 r.
Rel work on WY.
Join panels leaving one open seam.

WAISTBAND

(Knit two)
Bring forward 104 (112 120 128
136) ns.
With wrong side facing, gather 2
panels onto ns.
RC 000, MT-1, K 16 rs.
T10, K 1 r.
MT-1, K 16 rs.
T10, K 1 r.
C.off loosely.

TO MAKE UP

Join last seam, fold waistband to
inside and slip st into pos.
Thread elastic through waist.
Press.

Jacket

BACK

Insert card and lock to K row 1.
Col A, c.on in 1 × 1 rib, 109 (117
125 133 141) sts.

RC 000, T2/2, K 50 rs.
Trans sts to M/bed. Inc 1 st.
RC 000, MT, rel card and work
weaving patt.
Col A feeder 1, Col B weaving
yarn.
K 14 rs weaving.
* Pick up 6 loops all across row
and place onto n above, K 20 rs. *
Rep from * to * throughout
garments.
AT SAME TIME
K until RC reads 120 rs.
C.off 5 sts beg next 2 rs. *
Cont to K until RC 218 (220 224
228 230).

Shape neck
Push 68 (72 76 80 84) sts at left
into HP, or K back onto nylon
cord.
Note card row No.
Work on right side only.
Dec 1 st at neck next 8 rs.
24 (28 32 36 40) sts rem.
K 2 rs.
RC 228 (230 234 238 240).

Shape shoulder
C.off 6 (7 8 9 10) sts beg next and
foll alt rs. 4 times in all.
Leave cent 36 sts in HP.
Work left side to match.
Rel cent sts on WY.

FRONT
K as for back to *.
Cont to K until RC 198 (200 204
208 210).

Shape neck
Push 62 (66 70 74 78) sts at left
into HP or K back onto nylon cord.
Mark card row No.
Work on right side only.
Dec 1 st at neck next and foll alt
rs. 14 times in all until 24 (28 32 36
40) sts rem.
K 2 rs.
RC 228 (230 234 238 240).

Shape shoulders
C.off 6 (7 8 9 10) sts beg next and
foll alt r. 4 times in all.
Leave cent 24 sts in HP.
Work left side to match.
Rel cent sts on WY.

SLEEVES
Insert card and lock to K row 1.
Col A, c.on 1 x 1 rib, 49 (51 55 59
61) sts.
RC 000, T2/2, K 50 rs.
Trans sts to M/bed.
Inc 1 st.

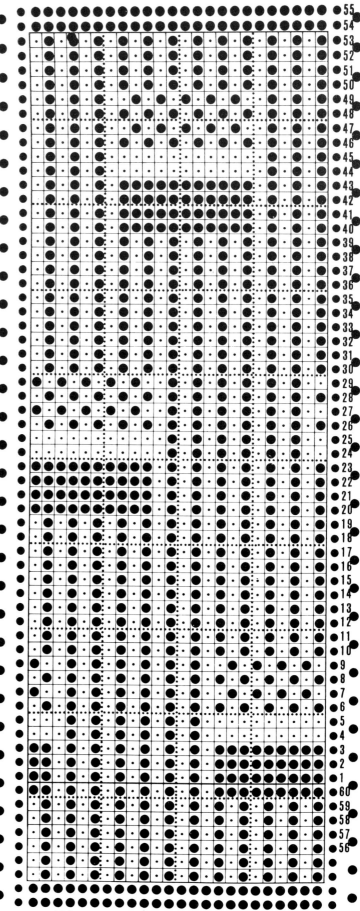

106

RC 000, MT, rel card and work in
weaving pattern. K 6 rs.
Inc 1 st both ends next and foll 5th
rs, until 118 (120 124 128 130) sts.
Cont to K until RC 192.
C.off loosely.

NECKBAND

Col A, c.on in 1 × 1 rib, 131 sts.
RC 000, T3/3, K 2 rs. T2/2, K 10 rs.
T1/1, K 8 rs. T2/2, K 10 rs.
T3/3, K 2 rs.
Trans sts to M/bed.
With wrong side facing, pick up sts
around neck, 52 sts across back,
30 sts from front shaping, 20 sts
held on WY at front, 29 sts from
front shaping.
MT + 1, K 1 r. T10, K 1 r.
C.off with latch tool.

TO MAKE UP

Join shoulder seams, insert sleeves.
Sew side and sleeve seams.
Fold neckband to inside and slip st
into pos.
Press.

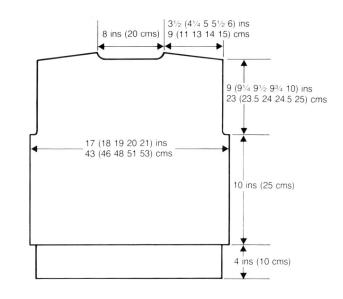

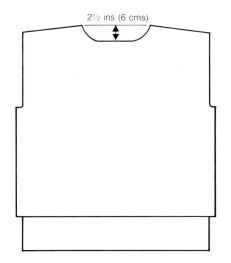

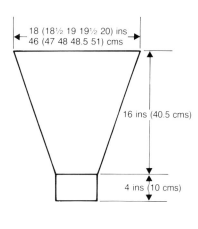

24 Shades of Green-Claret
FISHERMAN'S RIB JACKET SUIT

Sizes 32/34 (36/38 40/42) ins (81/86 (91/97 102/107) cms) bust
Skirt length 32 ins (81 cms)

Materials 2 Cones BK 4-ply Mohair: Col A
1 Cone Atkinsons 2-ply Pure Wool: Col B

Tension 28 sts × 48 rs = 4 ins (10 cms) using Col A over mohair rib pattern
Tension dials approx 7/7

37 sts × 50 rs = 4 ins (10 cms) Using Col B over skirt rib pattern
Tension dials approx 2/3

Skirt

(Knit 2(2 2 2 3) panels

Needle arrangement:
11111111111111   M/bed
11 111 111 111 Rib/bed (3 × 1 rib)

Col A, c.on in full n rib, 167 (178 186 198 70) ns.
Work c.on rs.
Trans sts from rib bed into 3 × 1 rib.
RC 000, MT, K 226 rs.
MT-1, on both beds K 18 rs.
C.off loosely.

TO MAKE UP
Join seams, 1 st each end.
Fold waistband to inside and slip st into pos.
Thread elastic through waist.
Press.

Jacket

BACK
Col A, c.on in 1 × 1 rib, 131 (143 155) sts.
RC 000, T6/6, K 4 rs.
Set carr for English rib, MT, K 240 rs.

Shape armholes
C.off 8 (10 12) sts beg next 2 rs.
Cont to K until RC 372.

Shape shoulder
C.off 7 (8 9) sts beg next 8 rs.
Rel cent 59 sts on WY.

FRONT
Col A, c.on in 1 × 1 rib, 67 (73 79) sts.
RC 000, T6/6, K 4 rs.
Set carr for English rib, MT, K 120 rs.
Mark pocket tops on 29th and 64th ns from left.
Cont to K until RC 240.

Shape armhole
C.off 8 (10 12) sts beg next r.
Cont to K until RC 341.

Shape neck
C.off 28 sts beg next r.
Dec 1 st at neck next and foll alt rs until 28 (32 36) sts rem.
Cont to K until RC 372.

Shape shoulder
C.off 7 (8 9) sts beg next and foll alt rs.
Rep for second side rev shaping.

SLEEVES
Col A, c.on in 1 × 1 rib, 85 (91 97) sts.
RC 000, T6/6, K 4 rs.
Set carr to K English rib.
Inc 1 st both ends next and foll 6th rs until 167 sts.
Cont to K until RC 256.
C.off loosely.

COLLAR

Col A, c.on in 1 x 1 rib, 117 sts.
RC 000, working in English rib, MT,
K 20 rs.
T6/6, K 10 rs. T5/5, K 12 rs.
T6/6, K 10 rs. MT, K 20 rs.
RC 72 rs.
Trans sts to M/bed.
With wrong side facing, pick up sts
around neck (not from c.off sts).
T9, K 1 r. T10, K 1 r.
C.off with latch tool.

POCKETS

Col A, c.on in 1 x 1 rib, 37 sts.
RC 000, T6/6, K 10 rs.
Set carr for English rib,
K 66 rs.
C.off loosely.

TO MAKE UP

Join shoulder seams.
Insert sleeves, sew side and sleeve
seams.
Sew pockets between markers.
Fold 4 ins (10 cms) at front neck to
form a revere.
Fold collar to outside.
Fold back cuffs.
Press very lightly.

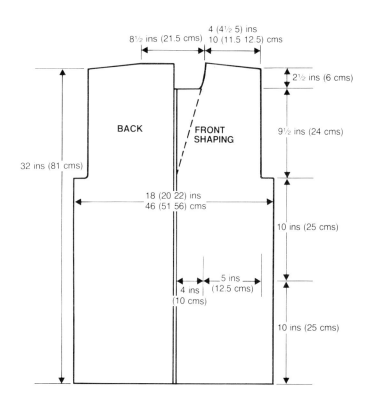

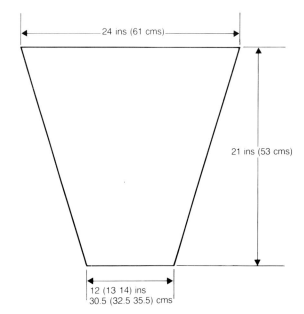

Evening

Sizes 32 (34 36 38 40 42) ins
(81 (86 91 97 102 107) cms) bust
34 (36 38 40 42 44) ins
(86 (91 97 102 107 112) cms) hip
Skirt length 30 ins (76 cms)

Materials 1 Cone Bramwell
Astrakan: Col A
250 gms matching Silky (2/30s
Acrylic Brights): Col A
Small amount lurex thread
2 small matching motifs

Tension 30 sts × 56 rs = 4 ins
(10 cms) using 1 end both Col A
Tension dial approx 3

Note Purl side is right side of
garment

Skirt

C.on in WY 195 sts.
K few rs, carr at left.
K 1 r with nylon cord.
RC 000, MT, using 1 end each Col
A, K 22 (26 28 34 36) rs.
* Push 125 ns left into HP.
Always taking yarn round last ns in
HP at left, push 5 sts into HP next
and foll alt rs. 13 times in all.
RC 26.
Push 5 sts at right back into WP
next and foll alt rs. 13 times in all.
RC 52.
K 42 (46 48 50 54 56) rs across
all ns.
RC 94 (98 100 102 106 108).
Bring 125 ns at left into HP.
Push 5 sts at left into HP next and
foll alt rs. 13 times in all.
Push 5 sts at right into WP next

and foll alt rs. 13 times in all.
RC 146 (150 152 154 158 160).
K 42 (46 48 50 54 56) rs across all
ns.
RC 188 (196 200 204 212 216).
Bring 125 ns at left into HP.
Push 5 sts left into HP next and foll
alt rs. 13 times in all.
Push 5 sts at right into WP next
and foll alt rs. 13 times in all.
RC 240 (248 252 256 264 278).**

Reset RC 000, work 5 more panels
from * to **.
K 22 rs.
Join back seam.
Pick up 1st row of knitting.

MT, K 1 r. T10, K 1 r.
C.off with latch tool.

WAISTBAND

Bring forward 104 (112 120 128 138
144) ns.
With K side facing, pick up sts
evenly from front or back waist.
MT, K 16 rs. T10, K 1 r.
MT, K 16 rs. T10, K 1 r.
C.off with latch tool.

TO MAKE UP

Join waistband and slip st to inside.
Thread elastic through waist.
Steam press.

SWEATER SUIT

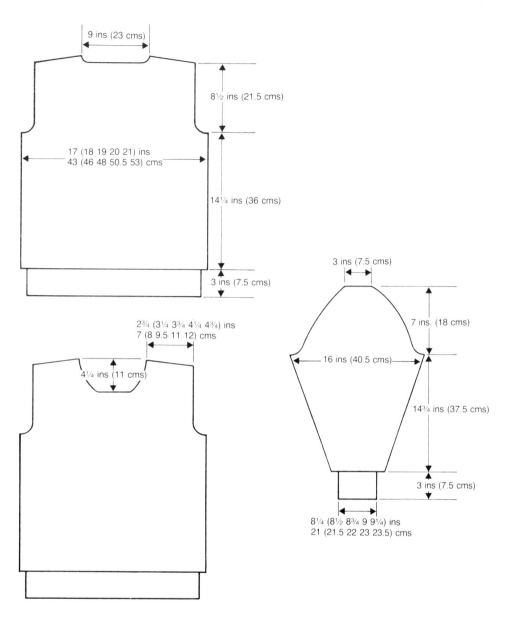

9 ins (23 cms)

8½ ins (21.5 cms)

17 (18 19 20 21) ins
43 (46 48 50.5 53) cms

14¼ ins (36 cms)

3 ins (7.5 cms)

2¾ (3¼ 3¾ 4¼ 4¾) ins
7 (8 9.5 11 12) cms

4¼ ins (11 cms)

3 ins (7.5 cms)

7 ins. (18 cms)

16 ins (40.5 cms)

14¾ ins (37.5 cms)

3 ins (7.5 cms)

8¼ (8½ 8¾ 9 9¼) ins
21 (21.5 22 23 23.5) cms

1 SKIRT PANEL

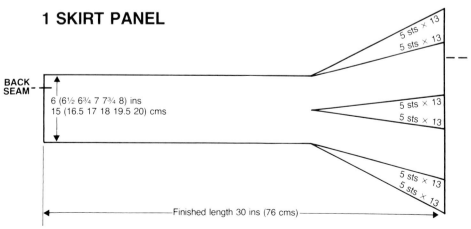

BACK
SEAM

6 (6½ 6¾ 7 7¾ 8) ins
15 (16.5 17 18 19.5 20) cms

5 sts × 13
5 sts × 13

5 sts × 13
5 sts × 13

5 sts × 13
5 sts × 13

Finished length 30 ins (76 cms)

Sweater

BACK

Using 1 end each Col A, c.on in
1 x 1 rib, 135 (143 151 159 167) sts.
RC 000, T0/0, using close knit bar,
K 36 rs.
Trans sts to M/bed, inc. 1 st.
RC 000, MT, K 200 rs.

Shape armholes

C.off 5 sts beg next 2 rs.
C.off 3 sts beg next 2 rs.
Dec 1 st both ends next and foll
alt rs until 116 (124 132 140 148)
sts rem. *
Cont to K until RC 320.

Shape neck and shoulders

Push 89 (93 97 101 105) sts at left
into HP. Work on right side only.
* C.off 4 (5 6 7 8) sts beg next r.
Push 1 st into HP beg next r.**
Rep * to ** 4 times in all.
C.off 6 sts beg next r and push 1 st
into HP at neck.
Leave cent sts in HP.
Push 27 (31 35 39 43) sts at right
back into WP.
Work right side to match.
Rel cent sts on WY.

FRONT

K as for back to **.
Cont to K until RC 260.

Shape neck

Push 79 (83 87 91 95) sts at left
into HP. Work on right side only.
Dec 1 st at cent next and foll alt
rs. 10 times in all.
Dec 1 st at cent next and foll 4th
rs. 5 times in all.
Cont to K until RC 320.

Shape shoulder

C.off 4 (4 6 7 8) sts beg next and
foll alt rs. 4 times in all.
C.off rem 6 sts.
Leave cent sts in HP.
Push 37 (41 45 49 53) sts at left
back into WP.
Work right side to match.
Rel cent sts on WY.

SLEEVES

Using 1 end each Col A, c.on in
1 x 1 rib, 65 (67 69 71 73) sts.
RC 000, T0/0, using close knit bar,
K 36 rs.
Trans sts to M/bed. Inc 1 st.
RC 000, MT, K 6 rs.
Inc 1 st both ends next and foll 6th
rs until 128 sts
Cont to K until RC 206.

Shape top

C.off 5 sts beg next 2 rs.
C.off 3 sts beg next 2 rs.
Dec 1 st both ends next and foll
alt r. K 1 r.
Dec 1 st both ends next and foll
4th rs. 20 times in all.
K 1 r.
68 sts rem.
C.off 4 sts beg next 2 rs.
C.off 3 sts beg next 12 rs.
C.off rem 24 sts.

PICOT NECK

Bring 156 ns into WP.
Pick up sts evenly around neck.
Using 2 ends Silky T3, K 4 rs.
Using lurex thread, K 2 rs. T9, K 1 r.
Trans every other st onto adjacent
n. T3, K 3 rs.
Silky K 3 rs. T10, K 1 r.
C.off with latch tool.

TO MAKE UP

Join shoulder seams.
Insert sleeves, gathering at top.
Sew side and sleeve seams.
Fold neckband inside and slip st
into pos.
Press.
Sew on motif.

26

Black EVENING SUIT

Sizes 32 (34 36 38 40 42) ins
(81 (86 91 97 102 107) cms) bust
34 (36 38 40 42 44) ins
(86 (91 97 102 107 112) cms) hip
Skirt length 30 ins (76 cms)

Materials 1 Cone Bramwell
Astrakan: Col A
250 gms matching Silky (2/30s
Acrylic Brights): Col A
Elastic to fit waist
Motif for top

Tension 32 sts × 56 rs = 4 ins
(10 cms) using 1 end both Col A
Tension dial approx 3

Note Purl side is right side of
garment

Skirt

C.on in WY 195 sts.
K few rs carr at left.
K 1 r with nylon cord.
Using 1 end each Col A, RC 000,
MT, K 22 (26 28 30 34 36) rs.
* Push 125 ns left into HP.
Always taking yarn round last ns in
HP at left, push 5 sts into HP next
and foll alt rs. 13 times in all.
RC 26.
Push 5 sts at right back into WP
next and foll alt rs. 13 times in all.
RC 52.
K 42 (46 48 50 54 56) rs across
all ns.
RC 94 (98 100 102 106 108).
Bring 125 ns at left into HP.
Push 5 sts at left into HP next and
foll alt rs. 13 times in all.
Push 5 sts at right into WP next
and foll alt rs. 13 times in all.
RC 146 (150 152 154 158 160).
K 42 (46 48 50 54 56) rs across
all ns.
RC 188 (196 200 204 212 216).

Bring 125 ns at left into HP.
Push 5 sts left into HP next and foll
alt rs. 13 times in all.
Push 5 sts right into WP next and
foll alt rs. 13 times in all.
RC 240 (248 252 256 264 278).**

Reset RC 000, work 5 more panels
from * to **. K 22 rs.
JOIN BACK SEAM
Pick up first row of knitting placing
sts over last row.
MT, K 1 r. T10, K 1 r.
C.off with latch tools.

WAISTBAND

Bring forward 104 (112 120 128 138
144) ns.
With K side facing, pick up sts
evenly from front or back waist.
MT, K 16 rs. T10, K 1 r.
MT, K 16 rs. T10, K 1 r.
C.off with latch tool.

TO MAKE UP

Join waistband and slip st to inside
Thread elastic through waist.
Steam press.

Sweater

BACK

Using 1 end each Col A, c.on in
1 × 1 rib, 135 (143 151 159 167) sts.
RC 000, T0/0, using close knit bar,
K 36 rs.
Trans sts to M/bed. Inc 1 st.
RC 000, MT, 196 rs.

Shape armholes

C.off 5 sts beg next 2 rs.
C.off 3 sts beg next 2 rs.
Dec 1 st both ends next and foll
alt rs, until 116 (124 132 140 148)
sts rem. *
Cont to K until RC 326.

Shape neck and shoulders

Push 83 (87 91 95 99) sts at left
into HP. Work on right side only.
Always taking yarn round last n in
HP, * c.off 4 (4 6 7 8) sts beg and
push 2 sts into HP at cent next r.
Push 1 st into HP beg next r. **
Rp. * to ** twice more.
C.off 4 (6 6 7 8) sts beg and push 2
sts into HP at cent next r. K 1 r.
C.off rem 6 (8 6 6 6) sts.
Leave cent 50 sts in HP.
Push 33 (37 41 45 49) sts at right
back into WP.
Work left side to match.
RC 335.
Rel cent sts on WY.

FRONT

K as for back to *.
Cont to K until RC 286.

Shape neck

Push 74 (78 82 86 90) sts at left
into HP. Work on right side only.
Push 1 st at cent into HP next and
foll alt rs. 20 times in all.
22 (26 30 34 38) sts rem.

Shape shoulders

C.off 4 (4 6 7 8) sts beg next and
foll alt rs. 3 times in all.
C.off 4 (6 6 7 8) sts beg next r.
K 1 r.
C.off rem 6 (8 6 6 6) sts.
Leave cent 32 sts in HP.
Push 42 (46 50 54 58) sts at left
back into WP.
Work left side to match.
Rel cent sts on WY.

SLEEVES

Using 1 end each Col A, c.on in
1 × 1 rib, 65 (67 69 71 73) sts.
RC 000, T0/0, using close knit bar,
K 36 rs.
Trans sts to M/bed. Inc 1 st.
RC 000, MT, K 6 rs.
Inc 1 st both ends next and foll 6th
rs until 128 sts.
Cont to K until RC 206.

Shape top

C.off 5 sts beg next 2 rs.
C.off 3 sts beg next 2 rs.
Dec 1 st both ends next and foll
alt r. K 1 r.

Dec 1 st both ends next and foll
4th rs. 20 times in all.
K 1 r. 68 sts rem.
C.off 4 sts beg next 2 rs.
C.off 3 sts beg next 12 rs.
C.off rem 24 sts.
RC 306.

NECKBAND

Using 1 end each Col A, c.on in
1 × 1 rib, 183 sts.
RC 000, T2/1, K 2 rs.
T1/1, K 2 rs. T0/0, K 24 rs.
T1/1, K 2 rs. T2/1, K 2 rs.
Trans sts to M/bed.
With K side facing, pick up sts
evenly around neck.
MT, K 1 r. T10, K 1 r.
C.off with latch tool.

TO MAKE UP

Join shoulder seams.
Insert sleeves, gathering at top.
Sew side and sleeve seams.
Fold neckband to inside and slip st
into pos.
Press.
Slip st motif to front.

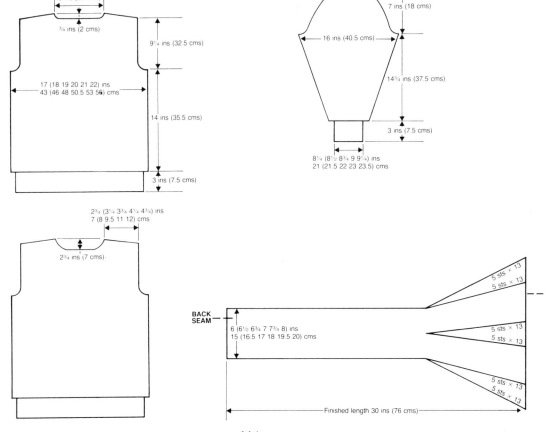

27

Turquoise
MOTIF TOP SUIT

Sizes 32 (34 36 38 40 42) ins
(81 (86 91 97 102 107) cms) bust
34 (36 38 40 42 44) ins
(86 (91 97 102 107 112) cms) hip
Skirt length 31 ins (79 cms)

Materials 1 Cone Bramwell
Astrakan: Col A
250 gms matching Silky (2/30s
Acrylic Brights): Col B
Elastic to fit waist
3 Motifs
1 spool Accent yarn (fine Lurex
thread)

Tension 32 sts × 56 rs = 4 ins (10
cms) using 1 end Astrakan, 1 end
Silky (Col A) over ss
Tension dial approx 3

Note Purl side is right side of
garment.
Wind Silky into 2 balls
(1 as Col A, 1 as Col B)

Skirt
C.on in WY 190 sts.
K few rs, carr at left.
K 1 r with nylon cord.
Always taking yarn round last ns in
HP, using 1 end both Col A, MT,
bring 170 ns at left into HP.
Push 10 sts at right back into WP
next and foll alt rs. 12 times in all.
Push 15 sts at right back into HP
next and foll alt rs. 4 times in all. *
RC 000, push 15 sts at left into HP
next and foll alt rs. 4 times in all.
Push 10 sts at left into HP next and
foll alt rs. 12 times in all.
Col B, K 2 rs across all ns.**
Bring 170 ns at left back into HP.
Push 10 sts at right back into WP
next and foll alt rs. 12 times in all.
Push 15 sts at right back into WP
next and foll alt rs. 4 times in all.
K 30 rs.*

Rep from * to * 12 (13 14 15 16 17)
times in all. Then from * to **.
Join back seam.
Pick up first row of knitting.
MT, K 1 r. T10, K 1 r.
C.off with latch tool.

WAISTBAND
(Knit two)
Bring forward 104 (112 130 128 136
144) ns.
With K side facing, pick up sts
from front or back waist.
MT, K 16 rs. T10, K 1 r.
MT, K 16 rs. T10, K 1 r.
C.off with latch tool.

TO MAKE UP
Join waistband, fold to inside and
slip st into pos
Thread elastic through waist.

Steam press.

Top
(Front and Back alike)
Using 1 end each Col A and Lurex
yarn, c.on in 1 × 1 rib, 135 (143 151
157 163 169) sts.
RC 000, T1/1, K 50 rs.
Trans sts to M/bed. Inc 1 st.
Remove Lurex thread.
RC 000, MT, K 144 rs.

Shape armholes
C.off 5 sts beg next 2 rs.
C.off 4 sts beg next 2 rs.
Dec 1 st both ends next r.
K 5 rs.
RC 154.
116 (124 132 138 144 150) sts rem.

Shape neck
Push 68 (72 76 79 82 85) sts at left

into HP, always taking yarn round last ns in HP at oppos end to carr, push 2 sts at cent into HP next and foll alt rs. 12 times in all.
Push 1 st into HP next and foll alt r.
RC 182.
22 (26 30 33 36 39) sts rem.
K 56 (60 64 68 70 74) rs.
RC 238 (242 246 250 252 256).
C.off rem sts.
Take carr to left.
Leave cent 20 sts in HP.

RC 154.
Work left side to match.
Rel all sts in HP onto WY.

NECKBAND
Using 1 end each Col and Lurex yarn, c.on in 1 x 1 rib, 135 (139 143 147 151 155) sts.
RC 000, T0/0, K 4 rs. T1/1, K 4 rs.
T2/2, K 3 rs. T4/5, K 1 r.
RC 12.
Trans sts to M/bed.

With knit side facing, pick up sts from front.
MT, K 1 r. T10, K 1 r.
C.off with latch tool.
Rep for back.

TO MAKE UP
Join shoulder seams and neck bands, sew side seams.
Work 2 rs double crochet around sleeve edges.
Press. Sew on motifs.

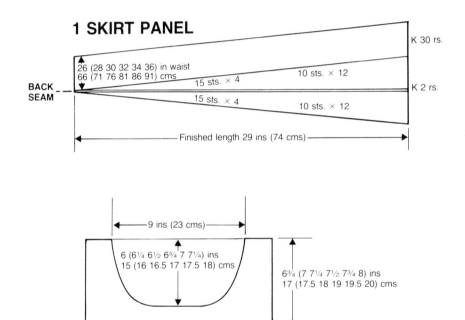

1 SKIRT PANEL

K 30 rs.

26 (28 30 32 34 36) in waist
66 (71 76 81 86 91) cms

15 sts. × 4   10 sts. × 12

BACK SEAM

15 sts. × 4   10 sts. × 12   K 2 rs.

Finished length 29 ins (74 cms)

9 ins (23 cms)

6 (6¼ 6½ 6¾ 7 7¼) ins
15 (16 16.5 17 17.5 18) cms

6¾ (7 7¼ 7½ 7¾ 8) ins
17 (17.5 18 19 19.5 20) cms

17 (18 19 20 21 22) ins
43 (46 48 50.5 53 56) cms

10¼ ins (26 cms)

4 ins (10 cms)

28

Cerise
SHIFT DRESS

Sizes 32/34 (36/38 40/42) ins
(81/86 (91/97 102/107) cms) bust
Length 43 ins (109 cms)

Materials 2 cones DB Matchmaker
2/3 ply
18 ins (45 cms) zip
1 motif

Tension 34 sts × 60 rs = 4 ins
(10 cms) over full needle rib
Tension dials approx 1/2

FRONT
Using fine/close knit bar, c.on in
full n rib, 147 (163 179) sts.
RC 000, MT, K 360 rs.
Mark both edges.
Cont to K until RC 480.

Shape armholes
C.off 5 sts beg next 2 rs.
Cont to K until RC 586.

Shape neck
Push 87 (95 103) sts at left into HP
or release from mach on WY.
Work on right side only.
Dec 1 st at neck next and foll alt
rs. 17 times in all, until 33 (41 49)
sts.
Cont to K until RC 630.

Shape shoulder
C.off 11 (13 16) beg next and foll
alt r. K 1 r.
C.off rem 11 (15 18) sts.
C.off cent 35 sts.
Work left side to match.

BACK
K as for front until RC 346.
Divide work for back opening.
Push all ns left cent 0 into HP or
rel. from mach on WY.
Cont to K as for front until RC 616.

Shape neck
K 1 r. C.off 27 sts beg next r.

Dec 1 st. at neck next 8 rs.
K 4 rs.
RC 630.

Shape shoulder
C.off 11 (13 16) sts beg next and
foll alt r.
K 1 r. C.off rem 11 (15 18) sts.
Reset RC 346, work left side to
match, casting off 28 sts.

SLEEVES
Using fine/close knit bar, c.on in
full n rib, 79 (87 97) sts.
* RC 000, bring every 6th n on
M/bed into HP, set lever on carr
to HP.
T2/2, K 4 rs.
Set lever on carr to K 1 r.*
Rep * to * 4 times in all.
RC 000, MT, inc 1 st both ends
next and foll 3rd rs until 171 sts.

Cont to K until RC 164.
C.off loosely.

COLLAR
C.on in full n rib, 155 sts.
* RC 000, bring every 6th n on
M/bed into HP, set lever on carr
to HP.
T3/2, K 4 rs.
Set lever on carr to K. K 1 r. *
Rep from * to * 4 times in all.
Insert fine/close knit bar.
T2/2, K 10 rs. T1/2, K 10 rs. T5/5,
K 1 r.
T1/2, K 30 rs. T5/5, K 1 r.
C.off loosely.

BELT
C.on in full n rib 12 sts.
RC 000, MT, K 100 rs.
Inc 1st next and foll 10th rs until
32 sts. K 200 rs.

Dec 1st next and foll 10th rs until
12 sts.
K 100 rs.
C.off loosely.

TO MAKE UP

Join shoulder seams, insert sleeves.
Sew sleeve and side seams.
Sew in zip.
Attach collar to neck.
Press lightly, sew on motif.

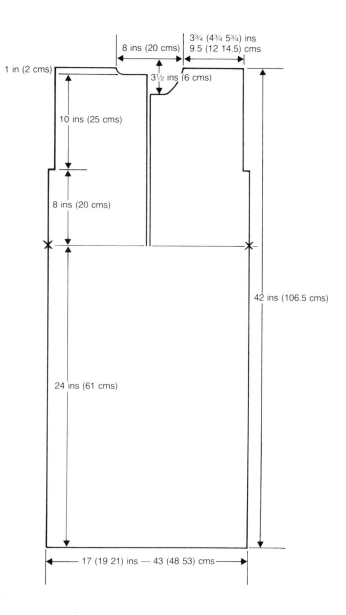

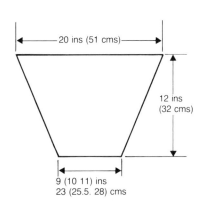

29

White MOTIF & BEAD SUIT

Sizes 32 (34 36 38 40 42) ins
81 (86 91 97 102 107) cms) bust
34 (36 38 40 42 44) ins
(86 (91 97 102 107 112) cms) hip
Skirt length 29 ins (74 cms)

Materials 2 Cones DB
Matchmaker 2/3 ply: Col A
Small amount 3/4 ply Lurex thread
2 shoulder motifs
1 Tube knitting beads
Elastic to fit waist

Tension 32 sts × 56 rs = 4 ins
(10 cms) using Col A over s/s patt
Tension dial approx 4

34 sts × 64 rs = 4 ins (10 cms)
Using Col A over full n rib pattern
Tension dials approx 1/2

Skirt
(Knit 2 panels)
Using close/fine knit bar, Col A,
c.on in full n bed rib, 154 (162 170
178 186 194) sts.
RC 000, MT, K 280 rs.
Mark both edges.
Dec 1 st both ends next and foll
8th rs until 112 (120 128 136 144
152) sts.
RC 442.
Mark both edges.
K 24 rs.
T8/8, K 1 r. MT, K 24 rs.
C.off loosely.

TO MAKE UP
Join side seam noting markers.
Fold waistband to inside and slip st
into pos.
Thread elastic through waist.
Press lightly.

Top
Counting from 4th n at left, c.on in

WY 112 sts.
K few rs to hang weights onto, carr
at left.
K 1 r with nylon cord.
Col A, c.on by hand over all ns, RC
000, MT, K 1 r.
Always taking yarn round last ns
in HP,

* Bring 104 sts at right into HP.
Carr at left, push 8 sts at left back
into WP next and foll alt rs. 13
times in all.
K 1 r.
RC 28.
K 14 rs. Carr at right.
C.on 80 sts (e method) at right.

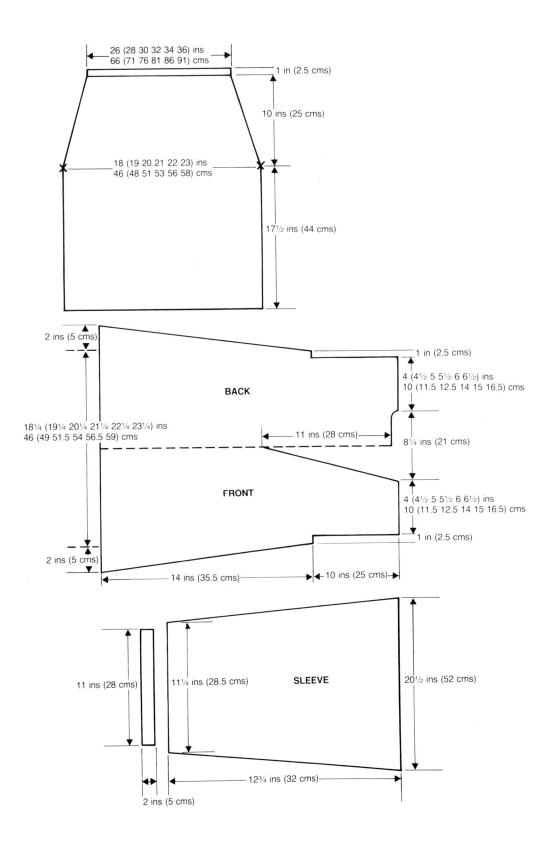

26 (28 30 32 34 36) ins
66 (71 76 81 86 91) cms

1 in (2.5 cms)

10 ins (25 cms)

18 (19 20 21 22 23) ins
46 (48 51 53 56 58) cms

17½ ins (44 cms)

2 ins (5 cms)

BACK

1 in (2.5 cms)

4 (4½ 5 5½ 6 6½) ins
10 (11.5 12.5 14 15 16.5) cms

18¼ (19¼ 20¼ 21¼ 22¼ 23¼) ins
46 (49 51.5 54 56.5 59) cms

11 ins (28 cms)

8¼ ins (21 cms)

FRONT

4 (4½ 5 5½ 6 6½) ins
10 (11.5 12.5 14 15 16.5) cms

1 in (2.5 cms)

2 ins (5 cms)

14 ins (35.5 cms)

10 ins (25 cms)

11 ins (28 cms)

11¼ ins (28.5 cms)

SLEEVE

20½ ins (52 cms)

12¾ ins (32 cms)

2 ins (5 cms)

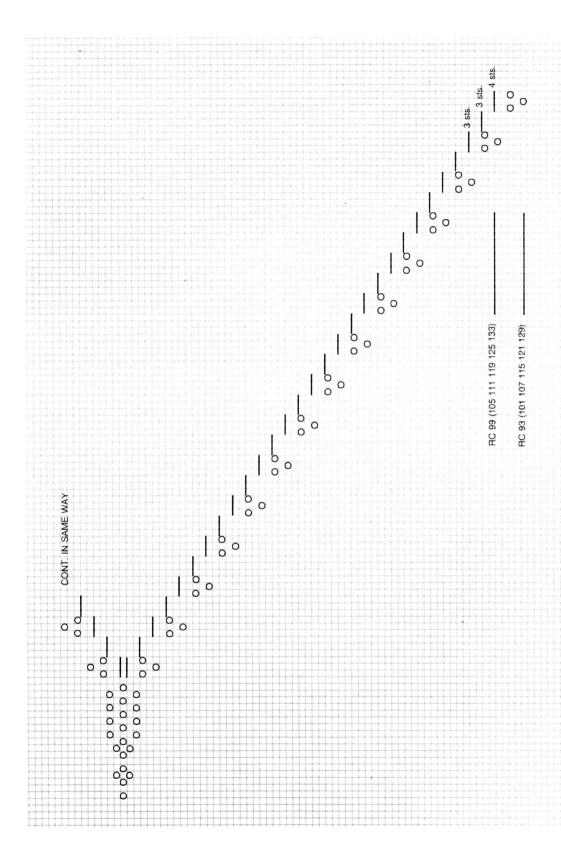

CONT. IN SAME WAY

3 sts.

3 sts.

4 sts.

RC 99 (105 111 119 125 133)

RC 93 (101 107 115 121 129)

SHOULDER

K 51 (59 65 73 79 87) rs. *
Work BEAD DESIGN from chart
and shape neck.
Counting from 3rd n at right, work
first bead into garment. K 2 rs.
Work 2 beads into garment. K 2 rs.

Shape neck

Work 1 bead into garment and
push 4 sts at right into HP. K 2 rs.
Keeping bead design correct, push
3 sts at right into HP next and foll
alt rs. 28 times in all.
RC 154 (162 166 174 180 188).
Rel sts in HP on WY.
C.on 3 sts at right next and foll alt
rs. 28 times in all. K 1 r.
C.on 4 sts at right next r. K 1 r.
RC 210 (218 224 232 238 246).

SHOULDER

Work 4 more rs bead design.
K 52 (60 66 74 80 88) rs.
RC 266 (282 294 310 322 338).
** C.off 80 sts beg next r. K 14 rs.
Carr at left, bring 8 sts at right into
HP next and foll alt rs. 13 times
in all.
RC 307 (323 335 351 363 379).
K 1 r. **

BACK

RC 001, mark left edge.
K as for front from * to *.
K 4 rs.
RC 97 (105 111 119 125 133).

Shape neck

Dec 1 st at right next 8 rs.
K 96 rs.
Inc st at right next 8 rs.
RC 210 (218 224 232 238 246).
K 56 (64 70 78 84 92) rs.
K from ** to **.
K 1 r. C.off loosely.

SLEEVES

Col A, c.on by hand 102 sts.
RC 000, MT, K 78 rs.
Always taking yarn round last ns in
HP, push 3 sts at left into HP next
and foll alt rs. 33 times in all.
Push 3 sts at right back into WP
next and foll alt rs. 33 times in all.
K 78 rs.
RC 288.
C.off loosely.

CUFFS

C.on in WY 88 sts.
K few rs, carr at right.
K 1 r with nylon cord.
RC 000, Col A, MT-1, K 8 rs.
T10, K 1 r. MT-1, K 8 rs.
Turn up hem.
With wrong side facing, pick up sts
from sleeve edge.
MT, K 1 r. T10, K 1 r.
C.off with latch tool.

HEMS

C.on in WY, 176 (176 184 184 192
192) sts.
K few rs, carr at right.
K 1 r with nylon cord.
RC 000, Col A, MT-1, K 8 rs. T10, K

1 r.
MT-1, K 8 rs. Turn up hem.
With wrong side of bottom edge
facing, gather sts from front or
back onto ns.
MT, K 1 r. T10, K 1 r.
C.off with latch tool.

CORD

C.on by hand in Lurex thread, 5
sts.
RC 000, MT-1, K 840 rs (approx 60
ins (150 cms)).
C.off.

NECKBAND: First Side

C.on with WY 144 sts.
K few rs, carr at right.
K 1 r with nylon cord.
RC 000, Col A, MT-1, K 6 rs.
T10, K 1 r. MT-1, K 6 rs.
Turn up hem.
With wrong side facing, pick up 78
sts from front, 66 sts across back.
MT, K 1 r. T10, K 1 r.

Second side

K as for first side with c.on 78 sts.

TO MAKE UP

Join shoulder seams, with open
edge at shoulder insert sleeves.
Sew side seams.
Using Lurex thread, work 2 rs
double crochet down sleeve edges.
Join sleeves by threading 3 beads
onto Lurex thread and sewing into
place.
Sew on shoulder motifs.
Press.

30

Pink
MOTIF
& BEAD SUIT

Sizes 32 (34 36 38 40 42) ins
(81 (86 91 97 102 107) cms) bust
34 (36 38 40 42 44) ins
(86 (91 97 102 107 112) cms) hip
Skirt length 29 ins (74 cms)

Materials 2 Cones DB
Matchmaker (2/3 ply): Col A
100 gms Silky (2/30's Acrylic
Brights): Col B
Motif for yoke
7 buttons
Elastic for waist
1 tube knitting beads

Tension 32 sts × 60 rs = 4 ins
(10 cms) over straight s/s
Tension dial approx 4

34 sts × 64 rs = 4 ins (10 cms)
Using Col A over rib patt
Tension dials using fine/close knit
bar T1/2

Skirt
(Knit 2 panels)
C.on in full n rib 154 (162 170 178
186 194) sts.
Work c.on rs.
RC 000, MT, K 280 rs.
Mark both edges.
Dec 1 st both ends next and foll
8th rs until 112 (120 128 136 144
152) sts rem.
RC 442.
Mark both edges.
K 24 rs.
T8/8, K 1 r. MT, K 24 rs.
C.off loosely.

TO MAKE UP
Join side seams noting markers.
Fold waistband to inside and slip st
into pos.
Thread elastic through waist.

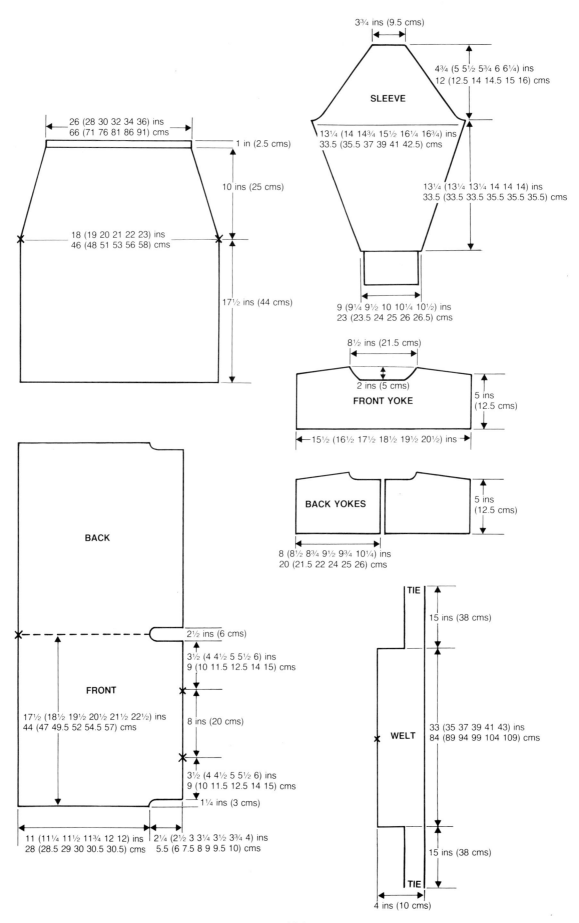

3¾ ins (9.5 cms)

SLEEVE

4¾ (5 5½ 5¾ 6 6¼) ins
12 (12.5 14 14.5 15 16) cms

13¼ (14 14¾ 15½ 16¼ 16¾) ins
33.5 (35.5 37 39 41 42.5) cms

13¼ (13¼ 13¼ 14 14 14) ins
33.5 (33.5 33.5 35.5 35.5 35.5) cms

9 (9¼ 9½ 10 10¼ 10½) ins
23 (23.5 24 25 26 26.5) cms

26 (28 30 32 34 36) ins
66 (71 76 81 86 91) cms

1 in (2.5 cms)

10 ins (25 cms)

18 (19 20 21 22 23) ins
46 (48 51 53 56 58) cms

17½ ins (44 cms)

8½ ins (21.5 cms)

2 ins (5 cms)

FRONT YOKE

5 ins
(12.5 cms)

15½ (16½ 17½ 18½ 19½ 20½) ins

BACK YOKES

5 ins
(12.5 cms)

8 (8½ 8¾ 9½ 9¾ 10¼) ins
20 (21.5 22 24 25 26) cms

BACK

FRONT

17½ (18½ 19½ 20½ 21½ 22½) ins
44 (47 49.5 52 54.5 57) cms

2½ ins (6 cms)

3½ (4 4½ 5 5½ 6) ins
9 (10 11.5 12.5 14 15) cms

8 ins (20 cms)

3½ (4 4½ 5 5½ 6) ins
9 (10 11.5 12.5 14 15) cms

1¼ ins (3 cms)

11 (11¼ 11½ 11¾ 12 12) ins
28 (28.5 29 30 30.5 30.5) cms

2¼ (2½ 3 3¼ 3½ 3¾ 4) ins
5.5 (6 7.5 8 9 9.5 10) cms

TIE

15 ins (38 cms)

WELT

33 (35 37 39 41 43) ins
84 (89 94 99 104 109) cms

15 ins (38 cms)

TIE

4 ins (10 cms)

Top

Purl side of bodice is right side of garment

BODICE

C.on in WY 88 (90 92 94 96 96) sts.
K few rs, carr at left.
K 1 r with nylon cord.
RC 000.
Col. A, K 2 rs. Col B, K 2 rs.
Col A, K 6 rs. Col B, K 2 rs.
Col A, inc 1 st at right next 6 rs.
Col B, K 2 rs. Carr at right.
RC 20.
Working Col A, K 6 rs; Col B,
K 2 rs:
c.on at right (e method), 14 (18 20 22 24 26) sts.
108 (114 118 122 126 128) sts.
Working in patt, K 60 (68 76 84 92 100) rs.
Mark right edge.
RC 80 (88 96 104 112 120).

CENTRE FRONT PANEL

Work 8 rs.
Work 8 rs of bead pattern as folls:
* (Working beads into cent st and every 10th st both sides cent, on 3rd row of next Col A, K 6 rs.)*
Work 16 rs. **
Rep from * to ** 6 more times, then rep from * to *.
Work 8 rs normal.
RC 210 (218 226 234 242 250).
Mark right edge.
K 60 (68 76 84 92 100) rs.

Shape armhole

RC 270 (286 302 318 334 350).
C.off 14 (18 20 22 24 26) sts at right.
Work 2 rs. Dec 1 st at right next 6 rs.
Work 12 rs. Mark both edges.
Work 12 rs. Inc 1 st at right next 6 rs.
Work 2 rs.
C.on 14 (18 20 22 24 26) sts at right.
RC 310 (326 342 358 374 390).
K 250 (266 282 298 314 330) rs.
RC 560 (572 624 656 688 720).
C.off 14 (18 20 22 24 26) sts at right.
Work 2 rs. Dec 1 st at right next

6 rs.
Work 12 rs. RC 580 (612 644 676 708 740).
Join seam, pick up first row of knitting.
MT, K 1 r. T10, K 1, r.
C.off with latch tool.

FRONT YOKE

C.on in full n rib, 132 (140 148 158 166 174) sts.
RC 000, MT, K 48 rs.

Shape neck

Push 87 (91 95 100 104 108) sts at left into HP or rel from mach on WY.
Work on right side only.
Dec 1 st at cent next and foll alt rs. 15 times in all until 30 (34 38 43 47 51) sts rem.
K 2 rs.
RC 80.
C.off rem sts.
Rep for left side.
C.off cent sts.

BACK YOKE

Col A, c.on in full n rib, 68 (72 76 80 84 88) sts.
RC 000, MT, K 64 rs.

Shape neck

C.off 31 (31 31 30 30 30) sts beg next r.
K 1 r. Dec 1 st at neck edge next 2 rs.
Dec 1 st at neck next and foll alt rs. 5 times in all.
30 (34 38 43 47 51) sts rem.
K2 rs.
RC 80.
C.off rem sts.

Work other side to match, working 1 r extra before shape neck.

JOIN BODICE TO YOKE

Bring forward 132 (140 148 158 166 174) ns.
With purl side of bodice facing, pick up sts between armholes, gathering where necessary.
With wrong side facing, pick up sts from front yoke.
T5, K 1 r. T10, K 1 r.
C.off with latch tool.

Join both pieces of back yoke onto bodice in the same way.

WELT BAND

C.on in full n rib, 12 sts.
RC 000, MT, K 200 rs.
C.on 28 sts at right.
K 500 (516 532 548 564 580) rs.
C.off 28 sts at right.
K 200 rs. C.off.

JOIN WELT BAND

Bring forward 132 (140 148 156 164 172) ns.
With K side of bodice facing, pick up sts to marker.
With tie end at right, pick up sts from shorter edge of welt band.
T5, K 1 r. T10, K 1 r.
C.off with latch tool.

Work other side to match.

SLEEVES

C.on in full n rib, 62 (66 70 74 76 80) sts.
Work c.on rows.
RC 000, T0/0, K 50 rs.
Inc 1 st both ends next and foll 6th rs until 106 (112 118 124 130 134) sts.
Cont to K until RC 200 (200 200 210 210 210).

Shape top

RC 000, c.off 5 (5 5 7 8 7) sts beg next 2 rs.
K 4 (2 2 4 4 0) rs.
Dec 1 st both ends next and foll alt rs until 40 sts rem.
RC 62 (66 72 76 80 82).
Dec 1 st beg next 10 rs.
C.off rem 30 sts.
RC 72 (76 82 86 90 92).

TO MAKE UP

Join shoulder seams.
Insert sleeves, sew side and sleeve seams. Make 3 loop buttonholes at back.
Work 2 rs double crochet around neck.
Sew buttons to back and sleeves.
Sew motif onto front yoke.

Postscript

As a dedicated hand knitter, making up my own patterns, my first encounter with a knitting machine 15 years ago was not exactly a case of love at first sight, all those wires and thingamajigs certainly put me off. Being fascinated by knitting I had to have a go, and like most new machine knitters I wanted to run before I could walk.

The first garments I knitted were a six panelled skirt with a fairisle top. I literally drove a friend to distraction with my cries for help, but by the end of the week I was proudly wearing my new suit and was hooked on machine knitting.

I now wanted to understand the machine and to learn how to use it properly so I set about working through the instruction book. The more I used the machine the more fascinated I became, the possibilities it offered for patterning seemed endless but as a beginner, wanting to practice all the basic techniques I had difficulty finding simple classic patterns, so I set about making up my own, resulting in a collection of patterns being published. Since that time I have designed and written patterns for other magazines and have edited an English version of an American knitting machine pattern book. I now spend all my time designing and writing patterns for knitting machines.

After all these years, machine knitting still intrigues me and I'm pleased to say I enjoy every minute I spend working on machines. I'm delighted to see more knitting machines are being sold than ever before and machine knitting continues to be one of the fastest growing leisure/hobby industries in Britain today.

I have been extremely lucky, my interest in knitting machines has taken me to America, Thailand and Japan where I was fortunate enough to visit Jones & Brother knitting machine schools. I have run knitting clubs and taught machine knitting. This has left me little time for my other hobbies which include oil painting, sketching, reading, tapestry, and embroidery. When I do have time to spare, I either listen to music or expend physical energy working out at my local gym or dancing.

Anyone who takes on the task of writing a knitting pattern book needs help and I am no exception, I am very lucky with the people who help me. I would like to thank Eileen Basketter who has carefully checked every pattern in this book. We have worked together for years now and have got to the stage where Eileen always manages to know what I am trying to achieve from the drawings and diagrams even when she may not understand my original written instructions, she really is a great help to me. I also have to thank her 'patient' husband Arnold, who has had to put up with late meals, a missing wife, and me, constantly interrupting what should have been quiet evenings at home.

My thanks must also go to Sue Steed who types my scribbles into legible reading matter for the printers. As Sue is also a machine knitter she understands what she is typing and can pick up all sorts of little things I may miss out.

I hope you will enjoy knitting and wearing the dresses and suits in this book, remember, if like me you can't always wear slim line skirts, you could knit one of the sideways knitted circular skirts to match the tops you like best, so giving you lots of different combinations. As long as you check your tension, most of these designs can be mixed and matched, even the punchcard designs can be changed to ones you may have a particular liking for, giving endless variations.

Photography by Tony Cambio

Models: Caroline Appleton
         Susan Harvey
         Yvonne Highton
         Mike Davies

Yarn Suppliers

YARN SUPPLIERS

Atkinsons Yarns
Terry Mills
Ossett
West Yorkshire
WF5 95A
England

BSK Ltd
Murdock Road
Manton Industrial Estate
Bedford
MK41 7LE
England

DB Designer Yarns
Moorland Mills
Law Street
Bradford Road
Cleckheaton
West Yorkshire
BD19 3QR
England

F. W. Bramwell & Co. Ltd
Unit 5, Metcalf Drive
Altham Lane
Altham
Accrington
BB5 5TU
England

KNITTING BEADS SUPPLIED BY

BSK Ltd
These Knitting Beads are available
in most good Machine Knitting
showrooms in England and
Overseas.

MOTIFS SUPPLIED BY

Beaded Motifs
3 Village Green
Canewdon
Rochford
Essex
SS4 3QF
England

OVERSEAS SUPPLIERS

Reynolds Bros
BK Yarns
53 Carlton Parade
Carlton 2218
New South Wales
Australia

Tessa B Knits
BK Yarns
Elna Sewing Centre
98A Norma Road
Myaree
West Australia 6154

Canadian Sole Importers
Bramwell Yarns
West Trade Sales Inc.
2711 No 3 Road
Richmond. B.C.
V6X 2B2
Canada

USA Sole Importers
Bramwell Yarns
PO Box 8244
Midland
Texas 79708
USA